Four Views on the Axiology of Theism

Also available from Bloomsbury

A Radical Pluralist Philosophy of Religion, by Mikel Burley
Debating Christian Religious Epistemology, edited by John M. DePoe and Tyler Dalton McNabb
Explaining Evil, edited by W. Paul Franks
Free Will and Epistemology, by Robert Lockie
God, Existence, and Fictional Objects, by John-Mark L. Miravalle
Sacred Music, Religious Desire and Knowledge of God, by Julian Perlmutter

Four Views on the Axiology of Theism

What Difference Does God Make?

Edited by Kirk Lougheed

BLOOMSBURY ACADEMIC
LONDON • NEW YORK • OXFORD • NEW DELHI • SYDNEY

BLOOMSBURY ACADEMIC
Bloomsbury Publishing Plc
50 Bedford Square, London, WC1B 3DP, UK
1385 Broadway, New York, NY 10018, USA
29 Earlsfort Terrace, Dublin 2, Ireland

BLOOMSBURY, BLOOMSBURY ACADEMIC and the Diana logo are trademarks of
Bloomsbury Publishing Plc

First published in Great Britain 2021
This paperback edition published in 2022

Copyright © Kirk Lougheed, 2021

Kirk Lougheed has asserted his right under the Copyright, Designs and Patents Act, 1988,
to be identified as Editor of this work.

For legal purposes the Acknowledgments on p. ix constitute an extension of
this copyright page.

Cover image © Pobytov / Getty images

All rights reserved. No part of this publication may be reproduced or transmitted
in any form or by any means, electronic or mechanical, including photocopying,
recording, or any information storage or retrieval system, without prior
permission in writing from the publishers.

Bloomsbury Publishing Plc does not have any control over, or responsibility for, any thirdparty
websites referred to or in this book. All internet addresses given in this book were
correct at the time of going to press. The author and publisher regret any inconvenience
caused if addresses have changed or sites have ceased to exist, but can accept no
responsibility for any such changes.

A catalogue record for this book is available from the British Library.

Library of Congress Cataloging-in-Publication Data

Names: Lougheed, Kirk, editor.
Title: Four views on the axiology of theism: what difference does God
make? / edited by Kirk Lougheed.
Description: London; New York: Bloomsbury Academic, 2020. |
Includes bibliographical references and index.
Identifiers: LCCN 2020020644 (print) | LCCN 2020020645 (ebook) |
ISBN 9781350083530 (hardback) | ISBN 9781350083547 (ebook) |
ISBN 9781350083554 (epub)
Subjects: LCSH: God. | Theism. | Values.
Classification: LCC BL473 .F68 2020 (print) | LCC BL473 (ebook) |
DDC 211/.3–dc23
LC record available at https://lccn.loc.gov/2020020644
LC ebook record available at https://lccn.loc.gov/2020020645

ISBN: HB: 978-1-3500-8353-0
PB: 978-1-3502-0564-2
ePDF: 978-1-3500-8354-7
eBook: 978-1-3500-8355-4

Typeset by Deanta Global Publishing Services, Chennai, India

To find out more about our authors and books visit www.bloomsbury.com
and sign up for our newsletters.

For Phillip H. Wiebe,
I miss you

Contents

Acknowledgments	ix

1 Introduction to the Axiology of Theism: The Current Debate and Future Directions
   Kirk Lougheed — 1

2 On Discovering God in the Pluriverse
   Michael Almeida — 19
   Commentaries on Almeida — 41
      Travis Dumsday — 41
      Perry Hendricks — 43
      Graham Oppy — 45
   Reply to Commentaries
      Michael Almeida — 50

3 The Axiology of Theism: Expanding the Contrast Classes
   Travis Dumsday — 59
   Commentaries on Dumsday — 79
      Michael Almeida — 79
      Perry Hendricks — 83
      Graham Oppy — 87
   Reply to Commentaries
      Travis Dumsday — 91

4 Skeptical Theism, Pro-theism, and Anti-theism
   Perry Hendricks — 95
   Commentaries on Hendricks — 116
      Michael Almeida — 116

	Travis Dumsday	120
	Graham Oppy	124
	Reply to Commentaries	
	Perry Hendricks	129
5	Naturalistic Axiology	
	Graham Oppy	137
	Commentaries on Oppy	157
	Michael Almeida	157
	Travis Dumsday	161
	Perry Hendricks	164
	Reply to Commentaries	
	Graham Oppy	168

Recommended Reading List	173
Notes on Contributors	175
Index	176

Acknowledgments

There are numerous individuals to thank when putting together an edited volume. To begin, I would like to thank Colleen Coalter at Bloomsbury. She was enthusiastic about my idea for this book from the very moment I first contacted her about it. Becky Holland at Bloomsbury has helped all along the way with administrative tasks (including helping me to stay on schedule!). I'm grateful that Bloomsbury was willing to give a junior scholar like me the opportunity to put together an edited collection.

I also must thank all of the contributors to this collection: Mike Almeida, Travis Dumsday, Perry Hendricks, and Graham Oppy. Many of them are far more senior in the field than I am and yet were excited to contribute to the volume and work with me. I'm humbled to have been the editor for their work. Given the interactive nature of this volume it was quite important that the authors meet deadlines. Not only did all of the authors meet the deadlines, but they also responded quickly to my emails. This made my job as editor much easier than it would have been otherwise. Perry Hendricks deserves special credit for joining the project rather late but still meeting all of the deadlines.

I would also like to thank Klaas Kraay. He sparked my initial interest in the axiology of theism and has been a constant source of encouragement. My parents, Stephenson and Diane, have always been supportive of my philosophical endeavors. I would not have gotten this far without them. This book is dedicated to one of my most important philosophical mentors, Phillip H. Wiebe. Sadly, he passed away in the fall of 2018 and did not live to see this book come to fruition.

Introduction to the Axiology of Theism

The Current Debate and Future Directions

Kirk Lougheed

The purpose of this introduction is twofold. The first is to provide a general overview of the literature on the axiology of theism. My hope is that readers unfamiliar with the current debate will not have to look elsewhere to situate the chapters in this volume. Second, I provide chapter summaries to better help the reader who may be looking for something specific navigate the volume.

1 Introduction: The Axiological Question about God

One important question in the philosophy of religion is the existential question of whether God exists. Arguments for the existence of God include the teleological argument, cosmological argument, and ontological argument, among others. Arguments for the nonexistence of God, on the other hand, include the problem of evil, the problem of no-best world, and the problem of divine hiddenness, among others. There are many variations of these arguments with much ink being spilled over them, sometimes going back many centuries. Other popular topics include the coherence of divine attributes, religious epistemology, and the cognitive science of religion.

In 1990, the highly prolific philosopher Nicholas Rescher touched upon a question about God that was seemingly different from the existential question. Rescher distinguishes between the belief that God exists and the desire that God exists. He seems to think that the latter reflects an axiological judgment. But his focus is on whether theistic belief makes life "suitably rewarding" and as such he leaves much unexplored. Still, Rescher's work gestured toward a new axiological question about God. This is the question of what value impact, if any, does (or would) God's existence have on our world?

Rescher's brief thoughts on this question went unnoticed by the philosophical community until Guy Kahane's groundbreaking 2011 paper, "Should We Want God to Exist?" While Kahane is aware of Rescher's work, he is most inspired by some enigmatic remarks from Thomas Nagel:[1]

> I want atheism to be true and am made uneasy by the fact that some of the most intelligent and well-informed people I know are religious believers. It isn't just that I don't believe in God and, naturally, hope that I'm right in my belief. It's that I hope there is no God! I don't want there to be a God; I don't want the universe to be like that. (1997, 131)

Kahane's paper expands on these comments and has prompted a number of philosophers to take up the axiological question about God. Specifically, Kahane argues that it's rational for someone to prefer that God not exist if her life would lose meaning if it turns out that God exists. A grant from the John Templeton Foundation held by Klaas J. Kraay at Ryerson University from 2013 to 2015 represents the first funded project solely dedicated to the axiological question about God. This resulted in both the first conference and the subsequent edited collection solely dedicated to the axiological question (Kraay 2018). It's safe to say that this has now become an established sub-topic in the philosophy of religion. The literature addressing this question is often referred to as the *axiology of theism*.

To date, the literature on the axiology of theism typically focuses on comparing the axiological implications of theism and atheism. More specifically, the axiological judgments tend to be between Judeo-Christian theism and ontological naturalism. Thus, the God in question is at least minimally construed as an omniscient, omnibenevolent, and omnipotent being who is creator and sustainer of everything contingent. On the one hand, the discussion oftentimes appears to presuppose a much more detailed conception of God, in particular, one closer to the Christian God. On the other hand, precise and agreed-upon definitions and usage of ontological naturalism are often difficult to find. But in the context of the axiology of theism literature it appears to refer to the idea that, minimally, God does not exist and more broadly that supernaturalism is false. The only causes which exist are natural causes. I will say more about expanding the relevant comparison classes in the conclusion of this introduction.

1.1 A Worry about Counter-Possibles

One might wonder whether the axiological question is worthy of serious philosophical reflection for the following reason: If God exists, then (many suppose) God exists necessarily. If God exists necessarily, then God exists in every possible world. But consider this: If God does exist, the world would be better (or worse). This is a counter-possible, and typically understood as trivially true (on standard Lewis-Stalnaker semantics). For if God exists then there aren't any possible worlds where God does not exist which we could compare to ours. There could be no cross-world axiological judgments, at least with respect to God's value impact. In his early piece, Kahane explains,

> We are not asking theists to conceive of God's death—to imagine that God stopped existing. And given that theists believe that God created the universe, when we ask them to consider His inexistence we are not asking them to conceive an empty void. . . . I will understand the comparison to involve the actual world [where God exists] and the closest possible world where [God does not exist]. (Kahane 2011, 676)

It is this comparison that Kahane and the subsequent authors exploring the axiological question have in mind. Still, it's noteworthy that while this makes the comparison Kahane has in mind clear, it does not address the counter-possible worry about the intelligibility of the axiological question.[2]

One solution to this worry proposes to stop understanding the comparison in question as one between *metaphysically* possible worlds. Rather, the relevant comparison should be understood as being between *epistemically* possible worlds. David J. Chalmers explains that something "is *epistemically possible* for a subject that p, when it might be that p for all the subject knows. A scenario is a maximally specific way things might be: a sort of epistemically possible world, in a loose and intuitive sense" (Chalmers 2011, 60). Chalmers continues,

> To fill out this picture, we might imagine that there is an overarching space of scenarios. These scenarios constitute *epistemic space*. If a subject did not know anything, all scenarios would be epistemically possible for the subject. When a subject knows something, some scenarios are excluded . . . it is

natural to hold that for a given p, there may be scenarios in which p is the case, and scenarios in which p is not the case. Then when a subject knows that p, scenarios in which p is not the case are excluded, while others are left open. The scenarios that are epistemically possible for a subject are those that are not excluded by any knowledge of the subject. . . . A scenario is doxastically possible for a subject if and only if is not doxastically ruled out by any of the subject's beliefs. When a belief qualifies as knowledge, the scenarios ruled out as doxastically impossible are also ruled out as epistemically impossible. (Chalmers 2011, 61)

I propose understanding what Chalmers refers to as a *scenario* as an *epistemically possible world*. Remember that the axiological question is intended to be distinct from the ontological question of whether God exists. Given that is irrelevant to the axiological question whether God in fact exists we can say that we are being asked to compare two different scenarios or epistemically possible worlds. The first is an epistemically possible world where God exists (and is as similar to the actual world as possible); the second is an epistemically possible world where God does not exist (and is as similar to the actual world as possible). Of course, if the former is true, then the latter world is metaphysically impossible. Likewise, if the latter is true, then the former is metaphysically impossible. Thus, the axiological question is intelligible when it is understood as a comparison between epistemically possible worlds rather than metaphysically possible worlds. In sum, "we are not dealing here with counterfactual space: the space of way things might have been. Here, we are dealing with epistemic space: the space of ways things might be" (Chalmers 2011, 62).[3] I won't spend more time on this here, but it's important to remember that throughout this volume the authors will sometimes continue to use the language of possible worlds, but keep in mind that this need not imply *metaphysical* possibility.[4]

1.2 Rational Preference versus Axiological Judgments

It's also worth noting that the literature on the axiologically of theism often treats rational preference as mapping on to axiological judgments. By this I mean that rational preferences and axiological judgments amount to the same thing. But it is an open question whether an agent's rational preference with respect to X need always correspond to her overall axiological judgments about *X*. In other words, perhaps it could be rational for an agent to prefer a less-than-best state of affairs. Kahane (2011) appears to think this is a genuine possibility. I won't dwell on this issue, but it's worth keeping in mind as one explores this topic.[5] We're now in a position to examine different answers that have thus far been proposed to the axiological question.

2 Possible Answers to the Axiological Question

Thus far, philosophers have focused most of their attention on two distinct answers to the axiological question about God. *Pro-theism* is the view that God's existence would or does increase the value of the world. *Anti-theism*, on the other hand, is the view that God's existence would or does decrease the value of the world. Of course, this means that someone who denies that God exists can be a pro-theist, while someone who affirms that God exists can be an anti-theist.

Recently, Kraay (2018) has observed that these are hardly the only two answers to the question. For instance, the *neutralist* claims that God's existence neither adds nor detracts from the value of the world. The *quietist* believes the axiological question is in principle unanswerable. And the *agnostic* holds that while the question is answerable, we currently ought to suspend judgment about it (Kraay 2018, 8). I'll refer to these five views as the general answers to the axiological question.

Each of these five general answers can be further subdivided. *Personal* judgments about the axiological question represent the value impact of (a)theism for persons. *Impersonal* judgments about the axiological question are about the value impact of (a)theism without reference to the value impact on persons. These personal and impersonal judgments can be applied to each of the general answers. The answers can also be divided based on narrow and broad judgments. The former refers to the axiological consequence of just *one* feature of (a)theism, while the latter concerns the axiological consequences of (a)theism *overall*. Personal/impersonal can combine with narrow/broad judgments to form some sixty possible answers to the question based on the five general answers I've identified. The below chart, which is very similar to Kraay's helpful chart,[6] enables us to visualize these different possibilities:

	Axiological Positions							
	Pro-theism				Anti-theism	Neutralism	Agnosticism	Quietism
	Impersonal		Personal					
	Narrow	Wide	Narrow	Wide				
Theism								
Atheism								
Agnosticism								

The pro-theism column contains all of the relevant subdivisions. Each of the other general answers can be similarly subdivided to contain all of the categories represented in the pro-theism column. In the following, I'll briefly explore defenses of pro-theism and anti-theism, which have been the focus of the literature thus far.

3 Defenses of Pro-theism

There are a number of different arguments that have been offered in defense of various versions of pro-theism, though to my mind many of them are significantly underdeveloped. Here are some of the arguments for pro-theism that I have in mind.

3.1 Any World with God Is Infinitely Valuable

Traditional theism typically assumes that God is a maximal being. That God is maximal is often associated with the idea that God is infinite, including being infinitely valuable. This implies that any possible world containing God is infinitely valuable. Since God is a necessary being, if God exists, *every* possible world is infinitely valuable. This line of thought provides support for wide impersonal pro-theism, since it establishes that God's existence is a good thing overall but without reference to individual persons. However, one might ask for more details about what it means to say that God is infinite. What does it mean to ascribe a number to God? It is literal or metaphorical? Likewise, some will protest that this argument leads to highly counterintuitive moral results. For instance, it implies that two possible worlds which contain vastly different amounts of pointless suffering turn out to have the same axiological value.

3.2 Morally Good Agents Add Value to States of Affairs

Another argument for pro-theism is based on the idea that morally good agents tend to add value to the states of affairs in which they exist (Penner and Lougheed 2015). The basic thought here is that God, as a supremely morally good being, necessarily adds value to any state of affairs in which God exists. This is different from the argument above about infinity because we aren't committed to the claim that every possible world with God is of the same value. The argument merely claims that God's existence always adds positive value.

3.3 No Gratuitous Evil

Related to the idea that morally good agents add value to states of affairs is the claim that there are a number of goods associated with theism. Identifying theistic goods, goods associated with the existence of God, and reflecting on their nature is another way to garner support for pro-theism. One such good is the idea that there is no gratuitous evil on theism. If this is right, then attempting to defend wide impersonal anti-theism is going to be extremely difficult. Kraay and Dragos observe that

> philosophers typically maintain that while it may be morally acceptable for God to permit some evil to occur, God cannot permit any gratuitous evil to occur: on theism, any evil that occurs is permitted either for the sake of obtaining a sufficiently significant, otherwise-unobtainable good, or for the sake of preventing a sufficiently significant, otherwise-unpreventable evil.... This is no ad hoc expansion of [theism]; instead, it is generally taken to be a logical consequence of the essential divine attributes of omnipotence, omniscience, and perfect goodness. (Kraay and Dragos 2013, 166–67)

The thought is that the impossibility of gratuitous evil is such a great good that it is likely that there is no atheistic good which could show atheism is better than theism overall. However, it's worth noting that some theists believe that the existence of gratuitous evil and God is compossible.[7]

3.4 Other Theistic Goods

A number of other theistic goods have been discussed in defense of pro-theism. Such goods include cosmic justice, an afterlife, and objective meaning and morality. Cosmic justice involves the idea that if God exists then there is a guarantee of cosmic justice. God's goodness entails that that wicked deeds will be punished and those who suffer will receive appropriate compensation. The pro-theist need not be committed to any details about how such justice is achieved. Though theism doesn't logically guarantee an eternal afterlife, many classical theists associate the existence of God with one. It is often thought that an eternal afterlife is a great good and adds value to the world. So its existence, if it is the result of theism, supports pro-theism. However, one may be skeptical about the positive value of an afterlife if it means that some humans will end up in hell. Finally, pro-theists may claim that without God there is nothing in which to ground objective morality and meaning. So if God exists, then the good of objective morality and meaning obtains, though we will soon see that some anti-theist arguments suggest certain individual's lives would lose meaning if it turns out that God exists.

4 Defenses of Anti-theism

It's now time to turn to defenses of anti-theism. Atheistic goods, goods associated with God's nonexistence, have been appealed to as a potential source of support for anti-theism. These goods are often connected to meaning in one's life. Thus, in what follows I will explain what has come to be known as the meaningful life argument in defense of narrow personal anti-theism. After this I will discuss atheistic goods disconnected from meaning.

4.1 The Meaningful Life Argument

Kahane is the first philosopher to explicitly gesture toward the idea that an individual could be rational to prefer that God not exist if it turns out that her life would lose meaning if God exists. He writes that "it might be that certain projects give our life its meaning and because of this it cannot be reasonable to ask us to give them up. If we did, we would no longer have a reason to live, perhaps no reason to do anything—including to care about morality" (2011, 691).[8] He continues,

> If a striving for independence, understanding, privacy and solitude is so inextricably woven into my identity that its curtailment by God's existence would not merely make my life worse but rob it of meaning, then perhaps I

can reasonably prefer that God not exist—reasonably treat God's existence as undesirable without having to think of it as impersonally bad or as merely setting back too many of my interests. The thought is that in a world where complete privacy is impossible, where one is subordinated to a superior being, certain kinds of life plans, aspirations, and projects cannot make sense. I suspect that certain actual life plans, aspirations, and projects that revolve around these values do not make sense, if the world is like that. (Kahane 2011, 691)

Here Kahane appears to be defending the rationality of narrow personal antitheism. He isn't claiming that God's existence would be a bad thing overall. He's merely stating that for individuals with certain values—the obtaining of which would be hindered by or impossible on theism—it's reasonable to prefer that God not exist. Kahane is unclear whether such values are intended to be objective (maps onto reality independently) or subjective (maps onto one's individual preferences), which we will see turns out to be important when evaluating the merits of this argument.

Myron A. Penner names Kahane's argument the "meaningful life argument." He develops Kahane's position in much more detail, though his purpose in doing so it ultimately to reject it. Many of Penner's worries about the meaningful life argument focus on the fact that people tend to be fallible at identifying and weighing goods that contribute to a meaningful life. We often think that when we achieve some end we will be happy and fulfilled, only to achieve that end and remain miserable (Penner 2015, 2018). He thus offers a version of the argument that appears to rely on one's subjective preferences with respect to what is valuable.[9]

4.2 Atheistic Goods Disconnected from Meaning

Also note that goods associated with atheism need not be connected to meaning in order to increase the value of the world. It's possible to recognize that something like privacy is a good independently from associating it with the meaning of one's life (Lougheed forthcoming). Other goods associated with atheism include things like solving problems without divine intervention, and bravery in the face of the unknown (i.e., atheism doesn't offer the same level of confidence as theism with respect to why we exist, and why we are here. At least this is so with respect to specific theistic religious traditions). One issue with attempting to defend anti-theism by appealing to atheistic goods disconnected from meaning is that it's unclear whether such goods could ever be valuable enough without such a connection to outweigh the theistic goods. More work needs to be done to identify and access the goods associated with both atheism and theism.

5 The Axiological Question and the Existential Question

Perhaps unsurprisingly, there are important connections between the axiological question and the ontological question. Specifically, in this section I will examine the connection between the axiological question and two arguments for atheism: the problem of evil and the problem of divine hiddenness.

5.1 The Problem of Evil

The problem of evil in view here is, roughly, that the existence of gratuitous evil makes it less likely that God exists, all else equal. For if God exists, then God would somehow ensure there was no (gratuitous) evil or at least ensure there would be a lot less than what we find in our world. Myron A. Penner and Benjamin H. Arbour argue that if someone endorses the problem of evil in defense of atheism, she must simultaneously endorse pro-theism—that is, if she endorses the problem of evil then she is committed to the claim that certain world bad-making properties (e.g., evil or gratuitous evil) cannot exist in a world with God (Penner and Arbour 2018). If Penner and Arbour are right, it means that an atheist like William Rowe, who famously championed the evidential argument from evil, is rationally required to be a pro-theist.[10] Penner and Arbour's argument, if successful, clearly establishes narrow pro-theism, since they point to respects in which the world would be better if God exists (i.e., no gratuitous evil). However, they think such considerations about evil are strong enough to establish wide pro-theism.[11]

While Penner and Arbour seem to focus on the evidential or probabilistic arguments from evil, Richard B. Davis and W. Paul Franks connect the axiology of theism to the logical problem of evil. They argue that Alvin Plantinga's response to the logical problem of evil (where he offers *possible* reasons for evil) is incompatible with his recent pro-theistic theodicy purporting to offer the *actual* reasons for why God allows evil (2018).[12]

5.2 Divine Hiddenness

There are also connections between the axiology of theism and the problem of divine hiddenness (2018a).[13] This problem assumes that if God exists, then God desires a loving relationship with all of his creatures. This is a great good and wouldn't be denied to a human who genuinely desired it. But, so the argument goes, there appear to be instances of non-culpable, nonresistant, nonbelief. So, God (probably) doesn't exist (Schellenberg 1993, 2015). It has been argued reflections on the axiological consequences of theism and atheism offer a possible solution to the problem of divine hiddenness. As noted earlier, goods associated with atheism include things like privacy, independence, and autonomy. These goods can be *experienced* on theism if God is hidden. For instance, an individual might feel as if she enjoys a high degree of mental privacy even if turns out she doesn't because God exists. Likewise, all of the goods associated with theism obtain in a world where God hides.

Of course, this argument is not meant to suggest that the experience of a good is axiologically equivalent to the actual obtaining of the good. Objections to hedonism indicate that experiencing a great life isn't all that matters if we wouldn't choose such a life knowing it to be a fraud (Williams 1981). Still, a world with a hidden God is the only one where one set of goods actually obtains along with the experience of the other set. There are at least two objections to this argument. The first is that there is a large value drop from a world where God isn't hidden to one where God hides. This is because there are theistic goods that only obtain in a world where God isn't hidden or obtain in a way quite different (i.e., they are more valuable) than how they obtain in world where God hides. The second is that it's intelligible to think that goods typically associated with theism can be *experienced* in a world where God doesn't exist (Hendricks and Lougheed 2019). If this is right, then an atheistic world can have theistic goods, making it difficult to see why we should prefer a world where God hides.

5.3 Anti-theism Entails Atheism

Another connection between the axiological question and the ontological question is the claim that the anti-theist is rationally required to be an atheist. Michael Tooley argues that if God exists, God necessarily brings about the better over the worse (2018). But if anti-theism is true, then God doesn't exist. This is because God cannot bring about a worse state of affairs then a better one. And if anti-theism is true, then theism is a worse state of affairs then atheism. If Tooley is correct then it turns out to be false that the existential and axiological questions are unrelated to one another. Relatedly, John L. Schellenberg contends that even one negative feature of theism (e.g., lack of privacy) is evidence for atheism. This is because it's logically impossible that any negative feature be associated with God (Schellenberg 2018).[14]

6 Conclusion: Expanding the Debate beyond Theism and Atheism

I close this introduction by noting that there has lately been metaphilosophical discussion about the current state of the philosophy of religion. Some of this discussion focuses on the charge that contemporary philosophy of religion is dominated by relatively conservative Christian philosophers (Draper and Nichols 2013, Draper and Schellenberg 2017). Much of these philosophers spend their time defending different aspects of Christian doctrine from criticisms. In light of this, some argue that the philosophy of religion is really Christian philosophy. And it turns out that much of Christian philosophy is dressed up Christian apologetics. Elsewhere I've argued that we should be hesitant to attribute religious motivations to philosophers without strong evidence for doing so. I've also argued that the motivation of a philosopher is distinct from the question of whether that scholar is making a genuine philosophical contribution (Lougheed 2018b).

Regardless of what one thinks about the merit of these accusations, it's true that the philosophy of religion is dominated by two worldviews: theism and atheism. Theism usually represents, broadly, the Judeo-Christian tradition. Atheism, on the other hand, is often mistakenly taken to be equivalent to ontological naturalism. The discipline has little interaction with the many nontheistic religious traditions and other nonreligious worldviews that aren't appropriately classified as naturalistic. This is a mistake. However, that this is a mistake doesn't necessarily imply that current work is wrong or misguided, but it does mean its scope ought to be expanded. As Yujin Nagasawa observes, "The problem of evil and suffering is a . . . good example of an issue which can be tackled collaboratively by scholars in distinct traditions" (2017, 46). He goes on to observe the very different understanding of evil and suffering which exist in the Eastern traditions. Such insights are currently underexplored in contemporary philosophy of religion.

Some philosophers of religion seeking to expand the field have offered nonnatural conceptions of the divine (broadly construed) quite different from theism. For example, J. L. Schellenberg defends a view he calls *ultimism* (2013). This is the idea that the divine reality is something ultimate in factual terms, value terms, and in its importance for us. This concept is too vague to attribute violations of our privacy to it. In this way, then, the vagueness of ultimism may actually make it more palatable than classical theism. Likewise, it offers us normative content that is perhaps impossible with naturalism. However, it's worth noting that built into Schellenberg's account is the idea of *deep time*. The human species is very young and there is much we have yet to discover about ultimism. Thus, any conclusions about it should be held tentatively. Finally, I don't intend this brief discussion to provide decisive reasons to favor ultimism over theism or atheism. My point is simply that this is one nontraditional view of the divine that is worthy of further exploration in the philosophy of religion in general, and in the axiology of theism in particular. Indeed, the very name axiology of *theism* suggests the field is too narrow in its focus.

Since the axiological question is relatively new in the philosophy of religion, it's not surprising that the debate has primarily focused on the axiological value of theism and atheism. Since the question is so new, sticking with these familiar categories is indeed still breaking new ground. But my hope is that the axiology of theism debate continues to grow and eventually transforms into the axiology of worldviews in general. I hope philosophers will start to assess the axiological value of the Eastern traditions and other nonnaturalistic worldviews. For there may well be methods for, or categories of, axiological assessment in those different traditions we have yet to uncover. I thus hope that this volume marks one of the early contributions to a topic that will help to expand the field of the philosophy of religion in a number of exciting ways. Indeed, Travis Dumsday's contribution to this volume on pantheism is just one example of the ways in which the axiological of theism literature can be expanded.

6.1 Chapter Summaries

In Chapter 2, "On Discovering God in the Pluriverse," Michael Almeida continues his well-known work on theistic modal realism. Almeida's main argument is to suggest that theistic modal realism is axiologically superior to alternatives because it enjoys theoretical advantages over its competitors. Specifically, "theistic modal realism affords an absolute explanation for the totality of creation" (20). Travis Dumsday asks whether the existence of hellscapes, really awful worlds, which are entailed by theistic modal realism nullify the glory of God's creation. Perry Hendricks suggests that while Almeida has successfully established narrow impersonal pro-theism, this isn't a significant accomplishment because any of the narrow positions are easy to establish. Graham Oppy offers a number of criticisms to Almeida's chapter including questioning the assumption that there is a "single time scale for the entire pluriverse." Oppy also wonders how God is meant to interact with (i.e., create) worlds that are supposed to be isolated. In his reply, Almeida clarifies a number of points regarding his position. For instance, we can do something about the evil in the actual world because, while it is necessary, it is not permanent. He also observes that hellscape worlds are a problem for any type of theistic modal metaphysics (hence the modal problem of evil). Finally, there are different ways of establishing narrow versions of pro-theism and these are not all equally valuable.

In Chapter 3, "The Axiology of Theism: Expanding the Contrast Classes," Travis Dumsday seeks to expand the axiology of theism beyond monotheism to pantheism. However, he notes early in the chapter that there are many different varieties of pantheism, so the task of expansion is complicated from the very outset. Much of his chapter is devoted to explaining why we should be skeptical of attributing the same value to the Absolute that we do to God. Dumsday ultimately concludes that we should be agnostics about the axiological status of pantheism. In his commentary, Michael Almeida shares his skepticism about being able to correctly assess the axiological status of something like the Absolute. He pushes this skepticism further by observing that polytheistic worlds don't promise to be valuable, so it's difficult to know whether this fact should count against them. Perry Hendricks suggests that a case for personal anti-pantheism might be made based on the idea that distinct persons technically don't exist on pantheism, only the Absolute exists.

Graham Oppy thinks that expanding the contrasting class should go even further than asking about other religions. For example, we should ask the general question of whether the universe having governance is a good thing. In his reply, Dumsday is sympathetic to general concerns about the coherence of pantheism but notes that there may be resources in analytic metaphysics that the pantheist can draw upon. All of the contributors seem to agree that much more remains to be said about this topic.

In Chapter 4, "Skeptical Theism, Pro-theism, and Anti-theism," Perry Hendricks argues that if skeptical theism is true, then anti-theism is difficult to defend but not pro-theism. Given the type of the skepticism associated with skeptical theism, one can identify an unsurpassable good associated with theism (everlasting life with God) but not with atheism. Oppy criticizes Hendricks by suggesting skeptical theism entails a broader and unpalatable skepticism. Dumsday suggests that Hendricks should clarify the terms of the debate since relying on the sort of afterlife described by Hendricks is explicitly Christian. Almeida worries that Hendricks's reliance on the standard analysis of evil (used by skeptical theists) entails that every intrinsically evil state of affairs is in fact not gratuitous, even when it could have been prevented. Hendricks responds that he is not committed to the skepticism oft attributed to skeptical theism since it's only meant as a way to block certain inductive inferences. He agrees the terms of the debate should be clarified and that doing so may help pave the way for further axiological comparisons between more varying religions and worldviews.

In Chapter 5, "Naturalistic Axiology," Graham Oppy continues writing from the naturalistic framework he has been developing throughout his career. Oppy claims that since he believes that necessitarian atheism is true, to ask whether we should want theism to be true is like asking whether we should want Santa Claus to exist. Almeida observes that the axiological question about theism or naturalism can be asked on the plausible assumption that we don't possess infallible knowledge about God's existence. Along similar lines, Dumsday notes that the axiological questions about theism and naturalism are different for the settled naturalist and for the agnostic or someone just leaning toward naturalism. Finally, Hendricks says that even if Oppy's framework is correct we can still ask about the axiological status of different fantasies, if not preferences. Oppy responds that he was careful throughout his chapter to note that it is irrational for *him* to want God to exist. He thinks God's existence is impossible.

But he never says this applies to every naturalist, including those who see God's existence as a possibility. Oppy also says that one such example of a settled naturalist participating in debate about the axiological status of God is the very chapter he has written, which stakes out a previously unmentioned position. Finally, Oppy explains that while he doesn't deny people can indeed have desires for impossible things, it doesn't follow they are reasonable in these desires.

Notes

1. While Kahane acknowledges Rescher's contribution, it appears his ideas were formed independently and prior to discovering the Rescher piece. See Kahane 2011, 679 fn. 10.
2. Joshua Mugg addresses this objection in his 2016 piece, "The Quietest Challenge to the Axiology of God: A Cognitive Approach to Counterpossibles." Mugg argues that such comparisons are possible via a process known as *cognitive decoupling*. This process occurs when an agent pulls information "from a representation and perform computations on that extracted information" (Mugg 2016, 448). For instance, we understand what Buggs Bunny is doing when he picks and a hole on the ground, places it on the wall, and steps into it even though doing so is impossible. I won't evaluate Mugg's proposed solution here.
3. Another underexplored solution is to appeal to impossible worlds to make the comparison.
4. For more on the counter-possible objection see Kraay 2018, 3–5.
5. For more on rational preference versus axiological judgments see Kraay 2018, 15–16.
6. This chart is very similar to the one found in Kraay 2018, 9.
7. For example, see Hasker 1992 and van Inwagen 2006.
8. Kahane says this idea is inspired from Bernard Williams's famous objection to utilitarianism. Williams thought that utilitarianism requires us to give up the very things that give life its meaning (2011, 691). See also Williams 1981, 14.
9. See my Lougheed 2017 for a reply to Penner.
10. See Rowe 1979.
11. Kraay and Dragos also discuss this idea (2013, 166–68).
12. See Plantinga 1974, 2004, 2009.
13. See also Dumsday 2016.
14. For more on connections between the axiological question and the ontological question see Kraay 2018, 13–14.

Bibliography

Chalmers, David. (2011), "The Nature of Epistemic Space," in *Epistemic Modality*, edited by Andy Egan and Brian Weatherson, pp. 60–106. Oxford: Oxford University Press.

Davis, Richard B. and W. Paul Franks. (2018), "Plantinga's Defence and His Theodicy are Incompatible," in *Does God Matter? Essays on the Axiological Consequences of Theism*, edited by Klaas J. Kraay, pp. 203–23. New York: Routledge.

Dumsday, Travis. (2016), "Anti-theism and the Problem of Divine Hiddenness," *Sophia* 55 (2): 179–95.

Draper, Paul and Ryan Nichols. (2013), "Diagnosing Bias in Philosophy of Religoin," *The Monist* 93 (3): 420–46.

Hasker, William. (1992), "The Necessity of Gratuitous Evil," *Faith and Philosophy* 9: 23–44.

Kahane, Guy. (2011), "Should We Want God to Exist?" *Philosophy and Phenomenological Research* 82: 674–96.

Kraay, Klaas J. (2018), "Invitation to the Axiology of Theism," in *Does God Matter? Essays on the Axiological Consequences of Theism*, edited by Klaas J. Kraay, pp. 1–35. New York: Routledge.

Kraay, Klaas J. and Chris Dragos. (2013), "On Preferring God's Non-existence," *Canadian Journal of Philosophy* 43: 157–78.

Lougheed, Kirk. (2017), "Anti-theism and the Objective Meaningful Life Argument," *Dialogue: Canadian Philosophical Review* 56 (2): 337–55.

Lougheed, Kirk. (2018a), "The Axiological Solution to Divine Hiddenness," *Ratio* 31 (3): 331–41.

Lougheed, Kirk. (2018b), "Religious Commitment and the Benefits of Cognitive Diversity: A Reply to Trakakis," *Sophia* 57 (1): 501–13.

Lougheed, Kirk. (2019), "On How (Not) to Argue for Preferring God's Non-existence," *Dialogue: Canadian Philosophical Review* 58 (4): 677–99.

Hendricks, Perry and Kirk Lougheed. (2019), "Undermining the Axiological Solution to Divine Hiddenness," *International Journal for Philosophy of Religion* 86 (1): 3–15.

Mugg, Joshua. (2016), "The Quietest Challenge to the Axiology of God: A Cognitive Approach to Counterpossibles," *Faith and Philosophy* 33 (4): 441–60.

Nagel, Thomas. (1997), *The Last Word*. Oxford: Oxford University Press.

Penner, Myron A. (2015), "Personal Anti-theism and the Meaningful Life Argument," *Faith and Philosophy* 32 (3): 325–37.

Penner, Myron A. (2018), "On the Objective Meaningful Life Argument: A Reply to Kirk Lougheed," *Dialogue* 57: 173–82.

Penner, Myron A. and Benjamin H. Arbour. (2018), "Arguments from Evil and Evidence for Pro-theism," in *Does God Matter? Essays on the Axiological Consequences of Theism*, edited by Klaas J. Kraay, pp. 192–202. New York: Routledge.

Penner, Myron A. and Kirk Lougheed. (2015), "Pro-theism and the Added Value of Morally Good Agents," *Philosophia Christi* 17 (1): 53–69.

Plantinga, Alvin. (1974), *God, Freedom, and Evil*. New York: Harper and Row.

Plantinga, Alvin. (2004), "Supralapsarianism, or 'O Felix Culpa,'" in *Christian Faith and the Problem of Evil*, edited by Peter van Inwagen, pp. 1–25. Grand Rapids: Eerdmans.

Plantinga, Alvin. (2009), "Transworld Depravity, Transworld Sanctity, & Uncooperative Essences," *Philosophy and Phenomenological Research* 78: 178–91.

Renewing Philosophy of Religion: Exploratory Essays. (2017), edited by Paul Draper and J. L. Schellenberg. Oxford: Oxford University Press.

Rescher, Nicholas. (1990), "Chapter 1: On Faith and Belief," in *Human Interests: Reflections on Philosophical Anthropology*, edited by Nicholas Rescher, pp. 166–78. Stanford: Stanford University Press.

Rowe, William, L. (1979), "The Problem of Evil and Some Varieties of Atheism." *American Philosophical Quarterly* 16 (4): 335–41.

Schellenberg, J. L. (1993), *Divine Hiddenness and Human Reason*. Ithaca: Cornell University Press.

Schellenberg, J. L. (2013), *Evolutionary Religion*. Oxford: Oxford University Press.

Schellenberg, J. L. (2015), *The Hiddenness Argument: Philosophy's New Challenge to Belief in God*. Oxford: Oxford University Press.

Schellenberg, J. L. (2018), "Triple Transcendence, the Value of God's Existence, and a New Route to Atheism," in *Does God Matter? Essays on the Axiological Consequences of Theism*, edited by K. J. Kraay, pp. 181–91. Routledge.

Tooley, Michael. (2018), "Axiology: Theism Versus Widely Accepted Montheism," in *Does God Matter? Essays on the Axiological Consequences of Theism*, edited by J. Kraay Klaas, pp. 46–69. New York: Routledge.

van Inwagen, Peter. (2006), *The Problem of Evil*. Oxford: Oxford University Press.

Williams, Bernard. (1981), "Persons, Character and Morality," in *Moral Luck*, pp. 1–19. Cambridge: Cambridge University Press.

2

On Discovering God in the Pluriverse

Michael Almeida

1 Introduction

One approach to assessing the value of theism focuses on the comparative value of theistic worlds. On the epistemic conditional approach, the question is whether it would be better *if we learned* that our world includes a God than if we learned that our world does not include a God.[1] These hypothetical possibilities are each ways the world might *actually be* rather than ways the world might have been. The comparison is between discovering that our world includes a God and discovering that our world does not include a God. Each of these discoveries is possible, for all we know, or at least for all we know for certain.[2]

The epistemic conditional approach might also ask whether it would be better if we learned that *the pluriverse*—the vast totality of metaphysical space—includes a God than if we learned that there is no God or no pluriverse or both.[3] The question about God and the pluriverse invites a variety of responses. There are, for instance, confirmed atheists who have insisted on the existence of many gods in the pluriverse. David Lewis, to take one example, was both an unwavering atheist and a polytheist:

> As Peter Forrest has pointed out, I am perhaps the most extreme polytheist going. If, as I suppose, a being does not have to satisfy some inconsistent description to be a god, then I take the number of the gods to be at least $\beth_2$. Unlike most polytheists, however, I think of this world we live in as entirely godless. (Lewis 1983, xi)[4]

There are $\beth_2$ gods in the pluriverse, on this account, but disappointingly there's not one god in our particular region of the pluriverse—not one actual god.

The greater disappointment on this view is that there is no maximally great being anywhere in the pluriverse.[5]

Of course Lewis's views on the nature of the pluriverse are not the last word. We might discover that Lewis was just mistaken about the nature of the gods in the infinite regions of metaphysical space. We might discover, for instance, that a maximally great being—an Anselmian God—exists *from the standpoint of* every world in the pluriverse. We could discover, for instance, that the best solution to the most persistent and intractable problems in philosophical theology includes the combined ontology of Ludovcian realism and Anselmian theism. Those are the best theoretical reasons for commitment to an ontology.[6] The discovery that an Anselmian God exists from the standpoint of every world is just the discovery that theistic modal realism is true. And theistic modal realism offers us theoretical advantages unmatched by the discovery of a host of lesser gods scattered throughout the pluriverse.

Among those theoretical advantages, theistic modal realism affords an absolute explanation for the totality of creation. The unique virtues of absolute explanations are completeness and ultimacy. The virtue of completeness ensures that every part or constituent of metaphysical reality is explained. Since explanation goes all the way down, there are no brute facts.[7] The virtue of ultimacy ensures that explanation terminates in a self-explained being, an unmoved mover, a necessary being, God. Ultimacy ensures that the *whole or totality* of metaphysical reality is explained, and not merely the proper parts, regions, or constituents of reality. Absolute explanations are theistic explanations that exemplify both completeness and ultimacy.

In Section 2 I introduce theistic modal realism and provide the theistic modal realist's explanation for the pluriverse. Absolute explanations—what Swinburne calls "the best sorts of explanations"—provide an explanation for everything, every region in the pluriverse, every possible world, and all possibilia. In Section 3 I consider Jonathan Bennett's modal fatalism objection. Bennett's intriguing proof purports to show that absolute explanations are too costly. Absolute explanations entail that there are necessarily no contingent objects, properties, events, propositions, or facts. Both Jonathan Bennett and Peter van Inwagen concur that the total loss of contingency is simply unacceptable. Theistic modal realism provides a simple solution to the modal fatalism objection.

In Section 4 I consider a recent objection to absolute explanations from the impossibility of divine ultimacy. I show that the objection from the impossibility of divine ultimacy fails assuming any logic as strong as S4. In logics as strong as S4, iterated explanations of ultimate objects are reducible—as they should be—to first-order explanations.

In Section 5 I consider a fascinating challenge from moral indifference according to which the total amount of good and evil in the pluriverse is necessarily unalterable. I argue that the objection wrongly infers that the total amount of good and evil is *permanent* from the fact that the total amount of good and evil is metaphysically necessary. Necessarily existing evils are certainly unpreventable, but they are nonetheless eliminable.

I conclude in Section 6 that theistic modal realism affords unmatched advantages that are easily worth the well-known ontological costs. Theistic modal realism permits an absolute explanation for the pluriverse that avoids the cost of moral indifference and the cost of modal fatalism. Theistic modal realism can also accommodate libertarian freewill the deliverances of modal imagination, and indeterminate quantum effects.

The discovery that the pluriverse includes an Anselmian God would be particularly welcome news. The Anselmian God provides explanatory completeness and intelligibility in the pluriverse. It is good news that there is an Anselmian God in what Klaas Kraay has called the *narrow impersonal sense*.[8] Everything that exists, occurs, or obtains in the pluriverse does so as a matter of divine necessity. The pluriverse—including our world—is the manifestation of the glory of the divine creator who creates in accordance with the principle of plenitude: everything that could exist does exist somewhere in metaphysical space. Most fundamentally, we have an explanation for everything that exists, occurs, or obtains in the entire pluriverse without any loss in freedom or contingency.

2 Theistic Modal Realism

Theistic modal realism envisages the totality of metaphysical reality as a vast concrete pluriverse. Possible worlds in the pluriverse are understood as causally and spatiotemporally closed or isolated individuals. Worlds are the mereological sums of spatiotemporally connected individuals. Worlds are not containers holding those individuals or substantive locations of those individuals. The mereological sum is itself a large individual, a world.

Not everything that exists in the pluriverse *exists in* a possible world. Theistic modal realism maintains that God exists *from the standpoint of every possible world* analogous to the way numbers, properties, propositions, and events exist from the standpoint of possible worlds. Each exists in the pluriverse; none exists in any possible world.[9] God is no doubt a concrete individual—unlike properties and propositions—but an individual that does not exist in any possible world. God's omnipresence is understood as presence throughout the pluriverse—existing from the standpoint of every possible world—without having any more specific spatial or temporal location.

What there is, in the most inclusive and least restrictive sense, is the pluriverse and all of its inhabitants. Everything that exists in the absolutely unrestricted sense *necessarily exists*.[10] It is true in every possible world that the very same things exist unrestrictedly. From the point of view of each world, the entire pluriverse is the widest, most inclusive domain of quantification: the content of the pluriverse is *what there is*. Indeed the pluriverse itself exists necessarily.[11] It is false that anything might have been different if we take "reality" to be the entire pluriverse—literally all of metaphysical reality. There are no grander and grander pluralities.[12] The totality of metaphysical reality exists necessarily.

Theistic modal realism takes as the object of God's creation *the totality of metaphysical reality*, all actualia and all possibilia. To the question, what did God create, the answer is *everything unrestrictedly*. Everything in the pluriverse—all of divine creation—is a vast concrete reality, and it all exists in exactly the same way. What exists could not be more plenitudinous than divine creation is—the glory of God is manifested in the vast creation of the pluriverse.

According to theistic modal realism, God *necessarily creates* the pluriverse. It is not a contingent matter that we have the pluriverse we have. It could not have been any different from the way it is. In particular, possible worlds could not have included any other individuals than those they do include. Nothing could have exemplified any properties other than the properties it does exemplify. Everything necessarily stands in the relations it does stand in. There is no alternative pluriverse—differing even slightly in the properties exemplified, objects existing, events occurring, facts obtaining, and so on—to the created pluriverse.[13]

If everything in the pluriverse really does supervene on the vast mosaic of point-sized objects and properties in worlds—perhaps it does—then theistic modal realism maintains that God necessarily creates the vast mosaic of point-sized objects, each *necessarily* exemplifying the properties they in fact exemplify and *necessarily* standing in the relations they in fact stand in. No part of that mosaic could have been even slightly different from the way it in fact is. There just is no alternative pluriverse that might have been created instead.

The account of divine creation in theistic modal realism is not vastly different from the accounts found in Spinoza and Leibniz. According to both Spinoza and Leibniz, the object of God's creation is the totality of metaphysical reality. Similarly, for Spinoza and Leibniz, the totality of metaphysical reality necessarily exists.[14] The difference between the existence of divine creation and the existence of God, on this account, is that God exists as a matter of *intrinsic necessity* and divine creation exists as a matter of *extrinsic necessity*. Theistic modal realism maintains similarly that God necessarily exists—exists from the standpoint of every world—and is essentially uncreated whereas the totality of created reality necessarily exists and is essentially created.

The argument that God—the maximally great being—provides the absolute explanation for the pluriverse is Leibnizian. But it does not depend on the contingency of the pluriverse or its inhabitants. In *On the Ultimate Origination of Things* and the *Monadology* Leibniz famously developed a version of the cosmological argument.[15] And in the *Principles of Nature and Grace, Based on Reason*, Leibniz offers a defense of that argument:

> The sufficient reason for the existence of the universe cannot be found in the series of contingent things, that is, in the series of bodies and their representations in souls.... Thus *the sufficient reason*, which needs no other reason, must be outside this series of contingent things, and must be found in a substance which is its cause, and which is a necessary being, carrying the reason of its existence with itself. Otherwise, we would not yet have a sufficient reason where one could end the series. And this ultimate reason for things is called *God*. (Leibniz 1714, 210ff)

There are, no doubt, various ways to formulate the argument that Leibniz suggests in this and other passages. But, restricting attention to contingent beings, the general form of Leibniz's argument proceeds from (P) there is a maximal, finite or infinite, collection of contingent beings to (C) there is a necessary being that is the sufficient reason for the maximal collection of contingent being (Oppy 2006, 119ff) According to theistic modal realism, all that is required in Leibniz's argument is an inference from (P') there is a maximal, finite or infinite, collection of *essentially created beings* to (C') there is an intrinsically necessary being that is the absolute explanation for the maximal collection of essentially created beings.

Essentially created beings might be contingent beings, but they might also be extrinsically necessary beings. As we noted above extrinsically necessary beings exist as a matter of metaphysical necessity, but they are also essentially created beings. Some essentially created beings are necessarily created. That is the account of divine creation defended in theistic modal realism. The pluriverse—the totality of actualia and possibilia—exists as a matter of metaphysical necessity and the pluriverse is also essentially created.

3 The Challenge of Modal Fatalism

Peter van Inwagen and Jonathan Bennett have argued for the intriguing thesis that absolute explanations entail that, necessarily, there are no contingent objects, properties, events, propositions, or facts. The total loss of contingency is the cost of absolute explanation. The arguments are deceptively simple. Jonathan Bennett's version assumes that P is the largest contingent conjunction verified in the actual world.[16]

> The question, "Why is it the case that P?" cannot be answered in a satisfying way. Any purported answer must have the form "P is the case because Q is the case"; but if Q is only contingently the case then it is a conjunct in P, and the offered explanation does not explain; and if Q is necessarily the case, then the explanation . . . implies that P is necessary also. But if P is necessary then the universe had to be exactly as it is, down to the tiniest detail—i.e. this is the only possible world. (Bennet 1984, 115)

Many responses to van Inwagen and Bennett's argument focus on the nature of explanation. Some current responses, for instance, argue that since p, q, r, . . . ⊢ P, or alternatively p, q, r . . . together ground P, the individual contingent propositions together to the left of the turnstile explain the conjunction P. So the explanation of P need not be a proposition that is not conjoined in P. p, q, r, and so on are all conjuncts of P, but taken together as unconjoined contingent propositions they explain P. Other responses deny that there could be an infinite conjunction of contingent propositions. But responses of this kind are, to say the least, explanatorily unsatisfying. What we expect from an explanation of P—the totality of metaphysical reality—is an answer to the question why P is true given the infinite number of alternatives P' that *everyone agrees* might have been true. What we expect is what Swinburne calls "the best kind of explanation":

> An *absolute explanation* of E is an ultimate explanation of E in which the existence and operation of each of the factors cited are either self-explanatory or logically necessary. Other explanations cite brute facts that form the starting points of explanations; there are no brute facts in absolute explanations—here everything really is explained. (Swinburne 2004, 97ff)

Absolute explanations are *not* causal explanations. In absolute explanations, C does not stand in any causal relationship to E.[17] The relation between explanans and explananda in absolute explanations is not fundamentally a logical relation, either. Absolute explanations do not claim that there's some modal system in which it is a theorem that $\vdash \Box(C \longrightarrow E)$ or that $\vdash \Box C$.[18] Rather, the relationship between C and E is a metaphysical relationship. The metaphysical relationship between C and E guarantees that there's no possible world in which it is true that C and ~E. Absolute explanations include the further metaphysical thesis that there's no possible world in which it is true that ~C.

Bennett's argument above depends on both metaphysical theses. If Q is the absolute explanation for P, then Q's metaphysical relationship to P ensures that $\Box(Q \longrightarrow P)$ and $\Box Q$. Bennett points up the fundamental feature of intensional operators to be closed under implication (Bennet 1984, 111).[19] So we arrive at the conclusion that Q is an absolute explanation for P only if $\Box P$. Since P is a maximally consistent set of propositions describing the totality of metaphysical reality, Bennett concludes that all of metaphysical reality is necessarily as it is. Paraphrasing Bennett, . . . if P is necessary then the universe had to be exactly as it is, down to the tiniest detail—that is, our world is the only possible world.

The argument from modal fatalism shows that the theoretical costs of absolute explanation is the total loss of contingency. There are no contingent objects, properties, events, propositions, or facts. The argument assumes of course that the proper explananda of Q is the actual world—every actually existing thing, every true proposition, every obtaining states of affairs, and so on—that requires an explanation.

In fact the proper explananda of absolute explanation depends entirely on one's ontological commitments. Most discussions of divine creation—including the discussion of Bennett and van Inwagen—simply assume that the proper explananda are contingent actualia of one sort or another. But theistic modal realists urge that the proper object of absolute explanation is the pluriverse as a whole. On this view, the ontological totality requiring explanation includes all actualia and all possibilia.

But if there is an absolute explanation for the pluriverse, then Bennett and van Inwagen would urge, the pluriverse and everything in it exists as a matter of metaphysical necessity. And indeed it does. The pluriverse and everything in it necessarily exists, there is no alternative pluriverse distinct from the pluriverse that in fact exists. And of course it follows that, since the actual world is one region of the pluriverse, the actual world and everything in it necessarily exists.

Given that the pluriverse exists necessarily and that, therefore, the actual world exists necessarily, how *could* theistic modal realism preserve contingency? There simply seems no room for contingency in the pluriverse at all and that seems to be the problem that van Inwagen and Bennett are so worried about.

On theistic modal realism, every world is necessarily the way that it is, but this is consistent with contingency in the pluriverse. The Eiffel Tower, to take an example of one part of our world, is necessarily as it is in the sense that nothing meeting the strictest or most rigorous standards of similarity to the Eiffel Tower could fail to have any of its actual properties. Nothing meeting the strictest standards of similarity to the Eiffel Tower could fail to have even its most minor and insignificant properties. In this sense, the Eiffel Tower has all of its properties essentially. When the standards of similarity are high—when we are speaking in the strict and philosophical sense—nothing in the pluriverse counts as being the Eiffel Tower except the Eiffel Tower.[20]

Nonetheless, we can truthfully say that it is a contingent fact that the Eiffel Tower is made of iron. We can truthfully say that it is a contingent fact that the Eiffel Tower is made of iron because we are prepared to accept lower standards of similarity according to which a tower made of plastic—a strictly nonidentical counterpart of the Eiffel Tower—in some region of metaphysical space counts as being the Eiffel Tower in that region.

All contingency arises from the accommodation of assertions that presuppose less than perfectly strict standards of similarity in the selection of counterparts. Our counterparts are our representatives—just those beings in metaphysical space that count as being us under some standard of similarity. Could Hubert Humphrey have been a poached egg? According to some extremely loose standards of similarity, there exist poached eggs in some regions of the pluriverse that count as being Humphrey. You accept that Humphrey might have been a poached egg only if you are prepared to accept such loose standards. But you don't have to accept those standards—and most folks are just not *that* accommodating. Could Socrates have been an alligator? Plantinga, for one, seems to think the answer is yes (Plantinga 1974a). With sufficiently low standards on similarity, there's a vast amount of contingency in the world. Those low standards are indeed what make contingent statements true.[21]

Having an absolute explanation does entail that the totality of metaphysical reality—including our region of metaphysical reality and everything in our region of metaphysical reality—is necessarily as it is. In the strict and philosophical sense, nothing could be even slightly different from the way it is. But absolute explanations do not entail that there is no contingency in the pluriverse. Contingency arises in the pluriverse—as it does for any view on the nature of metaphysical reality—from lowering the standards on representation.

As we noted above modal fatalism is not a problem for theistic modal realism. There is an absolute explanation for the pluriverse and so the pluriverse exists necessarily and is necessarily as it is. There is a necessarily true proposition—the proposition that God necessarily manifests his glory in the creation of the pluriverse—that entails the existence of the pluriverse and everything in the pluriverse. It is also true that the actual world necessarily exists and is necessarily as it is, since the actual world is one region of a necessarily existing pluriverse. But there is also a vast amount of contingency in the pluriverse. Virtually everything in the pluriverse could have been different in countless ways.

4 Can There Be Ultimate Explanations?

Steven Maitzen and John Morreall offer a fundamental objection to absolute explanations. Absolute explanations essentially terminate in a self-explanatory explanans but, according to Maitzen and Morreall, *nothing could be self-explanatory*. Maitzen argues as follows:

> Suppose that N is necessary rather than contingent, and suppose that E, the explanans for N, is the fact that N had to obtain, occur, or exist. Now, E—the fact that N had to obtain, occur, or exist—is one explanation, maybe the strongest possible explanation, for why N does obtain, occur, or exist. . . . Nevertheless, E must be distinct from N. Even if N and E are both necessary, they remain distinct, for E is a fact about N, whereas N can't be a fact about N even if N is itself a fact. To repeat: nothing succeeds as its own explanation, so any finite, noncircular explanation contains something unexplained. (Maitzen 2013, 252–71)

According to Maitzen, if E explains why N must exist, then E must be diverse from N. Further, E will require its own explanation E' such that E' is diverse from E, and so on. If the sequence of explanation is finite and noncircular then something is left unexplained. Morreall offers an analogous argument against a self-explanatory being:

> Postulating a metaphysical principle in God called his essence, which includes or causes existence, only push the request for explanation back one step further. It cannot be an ultimate answer to the question "Why does this thing have p?" "Its essence includes p" or "Its essence causes it to have p," for we can immediately ask, "Then why does this particular thing have this particular essence?" (Morreall 1980, 206–14)

According to Morreall, if the explanation for the necessary existence of an object a is that a essentially or necessarily exists, we still do not have an answer to the question of why a essentially or necessarily exists.[22]

Suppose we aim to explain why a proposition p is necessarily true or why some object G necessarily exists. There are of course modal and non-modal analyses of essential properties, and so modal and non-modal analyses of the natures of objects. Maitzen argues here that, as a matter of explanatory principle, if E explains a necessarily existing object N, then E ≠ N. But this proposed principle is false. Consider the proposition $\Box p$. What explains the truth of $\Box p$? According to Maitzen, "The fact that N had to obtain, occur, or exist is . . . maybe the strongest possible explanation, for why N does obtain, occur, or exist." So, it is plausible to answer that $\Box\Box p$ explains $\Box p$—the *necessity of* $\Box p$ explains $\Box p$. What explains the fact that p is necessary, then, is that p is *necessarily* necessary. That consequence in fact follows axiomatically from any logic as strong as S4. It is just a theorem for metaphysical necessity that ⊢ □p ⟶ □□p. But it is also a theorem of S4 that ⊢ □□p ⟷ □p. This theorem tells us that □□p and □p are logically equivalent formulas. Under standard assumptions about meaning and logical equivalence, the proposition expressed by □□p is identical to the proposition expressed by □p. So, though □□p explains □p, it is also true that □□p and □p express identical propositions. So, the proposition expressed by □p is explained by the proposition expressed by □□p, and since those propositions are identical, we should conclude that □p explains itself.

Note that the very same argument offered against Maitzen above holds, with suitable modifications, against Morreall. Essential properties are typically expressed as a narrow scope necessities, or necessities within the scope of quantifiers, as in (∃x)□Fx. On the modal analysis of essential properties, this proposition says that there's some x that is necessarily F or essentially F. The proposition (∃x)□(∃y)(x = y) is the typical way to express the proposition that x has the property of existing essentially. The proposition states that there is some x such that necessarily x is identical to something—in other words, x exists in every world.

Now, suppose x = God and that God essentially or necessarily exists. It follows by the S4 axiom noted above, ⊢ □p ⟶ □□p, that □(∃y)(God = y) if and only if □□(∃y)(God = y). So, we have the fact that □□(∃y)(God = y) explaining the fact that □(∃y)(God = y). But there is again the logical equivalence in S4 that □(□□(∃y)(God = y) ⟷ □(∃y)(God = y)). So, we know that the proposition on the left side of that biconditional is identical to the proposition on the right side of that biconditional. The right conclusion is that necessarily existing objects explain their own existence.

That's a consequence we might have expected. The essential properties of God—in particular, the essential property of necessarily existing—require further explanation only if God *might have* lacked that essential property. But it is necessarily false that □(∃y)(God = y) & ◊~□(∃y)(God = y) unless we assume some logic weaker than S4. In fact, the logic generally regarded as capturing metaphysical necessity is the stronger logic S5.[23]

Steven Maitzen and John Morreall argue that absolute explanations are impossible since nothing could be self-explanatory. Recall that Maitzen argues that E explains N only if E is diverse from N:

Whatever it is E that explains why N must exist must be diverse from N and such that E will require its own explanation E' such that E' is diverse from E, and so on. (Maitzen 2013, 256)

But this is false. We know that $\Box\Box p$ explains $\Box p$ and, in the logic governing metaphysical necessity, $\Box\Box p$ and $\Box p$ are logically equivalent. These sentences express the same proposition. This is best interpreted as entailing that explanations for necessarily true propositions are redundant. The proposition $\Box p$ is self-explanatory; it is equivalent to its own necessitation.

John Morreall argued that if the explanation for the necessary existence of an object a is that a essentially or necessarily exists, we still lack an answer to the question of why a essentially or necessarily exists. But this also is false. $\Box\Box(\exists y)(God = y)$ explains $\Box(\exists y)(God = y)$. The fact that God necessarily exists is explained by the fact that God *necessarily, necessarily* exists. But the additional explanation is redundant since $\Box(\exists y)(God = y)$ and $\Box\Box(\exists y)(God = y)$ express the same proposition. The proposition $\Box(\exists y)(God = y)$ is self-explanatory; it is equivalent to its own necessitation.

5 The Challenge of Moral Indifference

Theistic modal realism provides an absolute explanation for everything in the pluriverse without any cost in contingency. Discovering that the pluriverse includes a maximally great being would certainly be theoretically advantageous. But there remains an ingenious challenge to the value of a theistic pluriverse that has its initial formulation in Robert M. Adams:

> We may be moved by the joys and sorrows of a character known to be fictitious; but we do not really believe it is bad that evils occur in a non-actual possible world, or good that joys occur in a non-actual possible world, though of course it would be bad and good, respectively, for them to be actual. I think that our very strong disapproval of the deliberate actualizing of evils similarly reflects a belief in the absolutely, and not just relatively, special status of the actual as such. Indeed, if we ask, "What is wrong with actualizing evils, since they will occur in some other possible world anyway if they don't occur in this one?", I doubt that the indexical theory can provide an answer which will be completely satisfying ethically. (Adams 1974, 211–31)[24]

Adams's question concerns what is wrong with actualizing an evil under the assumption that the very same evil must be actualized somewhere in the pluriverse. There are credible answers to Adams's question. Let's focus instead on whether we have any reason to *prevent or eliminate* evils in the circumstances Adams envisages. The circumstances are analogous to those that arise for (at least some) multiverse theories of creation.[25] Multiverse theories offer a solution to a host of difficult problems in philosophical theology on the assumption that God *necessarily* creates every on-balance good universe. On this view, God necessarily actualizes the best possible world, which of course contains a multitude of universes.

Since everything in the multiverse exists necessarily, we know that every instance of good and evil exists necessarily. But not only is existence necessary; every property of every existing object is necessary. No actual event, object, or state of affairs—whether it is good or evil—could have been otherwise. It is a consequence of the multiverse account of creation that there is exactly one possible world, so there is no modal distinction between what is the case and what is necessarily the case.

Consider whether we should prevent or eliminate evil in the multiverse. There are at least two reasons why the answer is no. First, every evil in the multiverse is necessary to the greatest good—the greatest possible good is the total good in the multiverse. Second, every instance of evil exists necessarily. There's nothing we could do about the evil in the multiverse in any case.

We might discover that a maximally great being exists in the multiverse and necessarily created all of the on-balance good universes. The moral indifference objection suggests that this discovery would be very bad news. If we discover that the actual world is the way multiverse theorists describe it, then there is no ridding the world of the vast amounts of evil we find in it. All injustice and all wrongdoing, large and small, are evils we are permanently saddled with. It is impossible for things to get any better, since the total amount of evil exists necessarily. The prevention of evil is impossible.

There are equally good reasons for lamenting the fact that every instance of good in the actual world exists necessarily. The world cannot get any better than it is. We cannot add to the total amount of existing good—we cannot add to the good in our own lives or to the good in the lives of others—since the total amount of good that exists does so necessarily.

Theistic modal realism also faces the challenge of moral indifference. Every instance of good and evil in the pluriverse, speaking unrestrictedly, exists necessarily. There is a total amount of good and evil in the pluriverse—all possible goods and all possible evils—that also exists necessarily. Of course, it's not true that all evil is actual evil. A great deal of existing evil is located in non-actual regions of the pluriverse—some of those regions are near the actual world and some of them are very far from the actual world.[26] But good and evil do not gain or lose value as a function of their location in the pluriverse. It does not make an evil worse that it has the property of being actual, and it does not make an evil less bad that it has the property of being merely possible.

We might discover that a maximally great being exists in the pluriverse and necessarily created all of metaphysical reality. The moral indifference objection suggests that this discovery would be very bad news. If we discover that the pluriverse is as theistic modal realists describe it, then there is no ridding the pluriverse of the vast amounts of evil we find in it. Every instance of evil in the pluriverse exists necessarily—there is nothing we can do about it. It is impossible for things to get any better in the pluriverse. The prevention of evil is impossible. But what about discovering that every instance of good in the pluriverse exists necessarily? This again would be very bad news. The pluriverse cannot get any better than it is. We cannot add to the total amount of existing good in the pluriverse, since the total amount of good that exists does so necessarily.

The challenge of moral indifference presents a fascinating problem for theistic modal realists. There's an immediate response to the problem according to which we have no moral reason to prevent or eliminate evil that is not actual. What we have moral reason to do, on this account, is see to it that evils do not occur in our particular region.

The problem of course is that requirements of impartiality and neutrality constrain what counts as a moral reason. There are no impartial or neutral reasons for eliminating evil in our region rather than eliminating evil in other regions of the pluriverse. The moral indifference objection is that, no matter what we do, the totality of metaphysical space will include the same amount of good and evil. The moral reasons we have to eliminate evil impartially are self-defeating. The pluriverse is unchanged in overall value whether we impartially eliminate evil or not. In short, we cannot act in ways that improve the pluriverse, we have simply to acquiesce in the good and evil that exists.

There is another response available to theistic modal realists. It is true that every instance of good and evil in the pluriverse exists necessarily, but it does not follow that every evil in the pluriverse exists *permanently*. Permanentism is the temporal view that it is always the case that everything is always something (Deasy 2009, 2073–89). According to permanentism there is no time at which anything comes into, or goes out of, existence. Impermanentism is of course the negation of permanentism. It is the view that things sometimes come into and sometimes go out of existence.

The theistic modal realist response to the problem of moral indifference is that the good and evil in the pluriverse exists necessarily, but it does not exist permanently. There is a total amount of good and evil in the pluriverse, but it is not true that there is a permanent amount of good and evil in the pluriverse. The total amount of good and evil in the pluriverse at t need not equal the total amount of good and evil in the pluriverse at t'. Instances of evil are in fact eliminable despite the fact that every instance of evil is necessary. If, for instance, someone falls and breaks an arm at time t, it is true that the total amount of suffering in the pluriverse at t includes the suffering endured from a broken arm. That suffering in fact had to occur somewhere—indeed, in many places—in the pluriverse, but it does not have to occur permanently in the pluriverse. Mending the broken arm can reduce the overall suffering in the pluriverse at time t'.

Compare a Spinozistic, impermanentist world. In Spinozistic worlds—perhaps including the actual world, as Spinoza thought—the total amount of evil at one time is not equivalent to the total amount of evil at another time. Instances of evil come into existence and go out of existence like most other things in Spinozistic worlds. But every instance of evil in Spinozistic worlds exists necessarily—exists in every possible world. Instances of evil exist in every possible world since, if Spinoza is right, the actual world is the only possible world.

According to the moral indifference objection, it would be bad to discover that we inhabit a theistic pluriverse. If theistic modal realism is right, then every instance of evil in the pluriverse exists necessarily—there is nothing we can do about it. But the moral indifference objection is mistaken. It is true that the total amount of good and evil in the pluriverse is necessary. But it is false that the total amount of good and evil in the pluriverse is permanent. We can act in ways that add to the total amount of good in the pluriverse at a given time, and we can act in ways that reduce the total amount of evil. And that is consistent with the fact that the total amount of good and evil is necessary.

It's a very useful heuristic to take seriously the idea that our world might well be a Spinozistic world. If so, then the actual world is the *only* possible world. It follows immediately that everything that happens here does so necessarily. Nothing could be otherwise since there are no other possibilities. But everything would appear just as it does to us right now if we indeed discovered that our world was Spinozistic. We could still eliminate evils, reduce suffering, and increase happiness, despite the fact that all the good and evil that occurs, exists, or obtains does so necessarily. The goods and evils are all necessary, but they are not *permanent*. We can alter the total amount of each at any moment. The same is true of the pluriverse. There is a unique total amount of good and evil in the pluriverse, but there need not be the same amount of good and evil at each moment.

6 Conclusions

Theistic modal realism permits an absolute explanation for the pluriverse that avoids the cost of modal fatalism and the cost of moral indifference. According to theistic modal realism there exists a maximally great being that is the ultimate explanation for everything in the pluriverse. As we should expect, the totality of modal space is necessarily as it is—this is indeed true on every account of modal space. Contingency in modal space is a consequence of the representation of objects, events, and states of affairs across possible worlds. Theistic modal realism licenses various, more or less strict, standards of representation and correspondingly various degrees of contingency.

The moral indifference challenge affirms that the total amount of good and evil in the pluriverse exists necessarily—there is nothing we can do to increase the total amount of good or decrease the total amount of evil. According to the challenge, discovering that theistic modal realism is true is bad news. It requires that we acquiesce in the amount of good and evil we find in the pluriverse. But the moral indifference challenge is mistaken. The total amount of good and evil in the pluriverse is necessary but not permanent. We can act in ways that add to the total amount of good in the pluriverse, and we can act in ways that reduce the total amount of evil. And that is consistent with the fact that the total amount of good and evil is necessary.

Discovering that there exists an Anselmian God in the pluriverse is good news in the narrow impersonal sense.[27] The Anselmian pluriverse is the manifestation of the glory of the divine creator who creates in accordance with the principle of plenitude. Everything that could exist does exist. In the Anselmian pluriverse we have an absolute explanation for everything that exists, occurs, or obtains in the entire pluriverse without any loss in freedom or contingency.[28]

Notes

1 The conditional in these cases is the material conditional, $p \supset q$, and not the counterfactual conditional. We are asking about the epistemic possibility that the pluriverse/world includes a god rather than the metaphysical possibility that the pluriverse/world includes a god. It is common to frame the question as a comparative counterfactual. On the comparative counterfactual approach the question is whether it would it be better were God to exist than it would be were God not to exist. But the counterfactual formulation is terribly misleading. If God exists, then there simply is no way things would have been had God not existed. The alleged counterfactual comparison is really a comparison between the value of the way things in fact are and the value of the closest impossible world. It is at least difficult to know what criteria determine the similarity of impossible worlds to the actual world. Do all impossible worlds explode? Is the logic of impossible worlds nonclassical or perhaps not even an extension of classical logic? The logical and metaphysical obstacles to assessing such counterpossibles are, I think, serious enough to undercut any conclusion on the axiology of theism.

2 I have in mind here *for all we know a priori*, but this broad notion of epistemic possibility is not required for the argument to follow. We might restrict what is epistemically possible to what is possible, for all we know *a priori* and *a posteriori* or for all we are certain of, or for all we justifiably believe. Compare Chalmers 2002.

3 Metaphysical space includes every possible world and all possibilia. For actualist realism (compare for instance, Plantinga, Stalnaker, and van Inwagen) the totality of metaphysical space includes only actualia, the actual world, and everything in the actual world. For genuine modal realists, metaphysical space includes a vast number of spatiotemporally isolated concrete worlds and everything inhabiting

4. those worlds. It includes in addition ontological items that exist in no possible world at all: numbers, sets, propositions, and, according to theistic modal realists, God.
4. It might be worth mentioning a discussion with Peter Forrest on the probability that a god actually exists given Lewis's pluriverse. $\beth_2 = P(P(N)) =$ the cardinality of possible worlds. We found that, for Lewis, there is about a 1/e chance that there is no actual god. That is, given just the number of gods and the number of worlds, the chances are about 65 percent that one of those gods is actual. There is of course other evidence both for and against the existence of the Lewisian gods.
5. It is certainly David Lewis's view that there exists no traditional God. One obstacle for Lewis is that the traditional God would have all of its essential properties as a matter of absolute necessity—God exemplifies the divine attributes in a metaphysically serious way. It is not a contextual matter whether the traditional God exemplifies perfect goodness, for instance. But Lewis also rejects the position that the traditional God can be consistently described. See Lewis 1970; See also Lewis 2015.
6. There's an argument for this conclusion in Almeida 2017a, b.
7. Compare Earman 1986. According to Earman causal determinism explains physical events all the way down, every single thing that happens, the way it happens, in total detail. Absolute explanations also explain all the way down.
8. See Kraay 2018.
9. See Cameron 2009: 97 ff.
10. "Everything" in the unrestricted sense is a quantifier whose domain is the entire pluriverse. So, "everything exists necessarily," when used unrestricted, means everything in the pluriverse—not just everything in our spatiotemporally isolated universe—exists necessarily.
11. I'm noncommittal on the issue of whether the pluriverse is itself an individual, another concrete mereological sum. I'm also noncommittal on the issue of whether there are individuals that are sums of worlds w and w' that are smaller than the pluriverse but larger than individual worlds. But there are metaphysical uses for both views.
12. Bryan Skyrms offers a regress argument that there must be larger and larger pluriverses. See Skyrms 1976. Compare Lewis 2001: 101 n. 1.
13. This can seem more radical than it is. There is no coherent account of possible worlds according to which the totality of possible worlds might have been different from the way it is. The most widely accepted account of the nature of possible worlds maintains that possible worlds are abstract objects of some kind, either states of affairs or propositions or properties, or the like. Suppose

we take possible worlds to be maximally consistent states of affairs. Could any possible world be any different from the way it is? No, every possible world exists necessarily—every possible world exists in every other possible world—and has all of its states of affairs essentially. So, every possible world is necessarily as it is, it could not be any different. Further, it is not possible to add or subtract from the number possible worlds that exist.

14 Both Leibniz and Spinoza were necessitarians, on the reading I am proposing. Both maintained that the actual world was the only metaphysically possible world and that the only intrinsically necessary being was God. Possible, non-actual worlds, for Leibniz, are intrinsically possible, but metaphysically impossible objects. For Leibniz this amounts to the view that there is no internal contradiction in the proposition that some other possible world is actualized, but those worlds are inconsistent with the existence of God. See Griffin 2013.

15 See Leibniz 1697; Garber 1989. See also Leibniz 1710, 1714.

16 Peter van Inwagen comes to the same conclusion in a very similar argument.

Someone might suggest, for example, that the actual future became actual not for any reason to be found in the natural world but rather because God chose that it should, God's choice being in that case the sufficient reason demanded by (the principle of sufficient reason [PSR]). However, PSR must be rejected, for it has an absurd consequence: the collapse of all modal distinctions. See van Inwagen 1983, 202–4, 2009, 150ff.

17 The relationship between C and E is fundamentally a metaphysical relationship. C metaphysically necessitates E, whether or not there are any causal laws. So C does not cause E.

18 For fascinating discussion of fallacious ways of reasoning about what might have been, Salmon 1989, 3–34. Salmon's arguments are largely aimed to show that true metaphysical theses—theses concerning material composition, for instance—are violated in some familiar modal logics. But of course it is also true that some necessary metaphysical theses are not provable in some widely accepted, sound, and complete modal logics.

19 What follows from something necessary is itself necessary, which is the most fundamental theorem of any modal logic. David Lewis makes a similar observation about closure governing intensional operators in 1978, 39ff. I have already noted that truth in a given fiction is closed under implication. Such closure is the earmark of an operator of relative necessity, an intensional operator that may be analyzed as a restricted universal quantifier over possible worlds.

20 But why is this the strict and philosophical sense? It is the only sense which strictly observes Leibniz's laws. Leibniz's laws entail that, for any x, y, x = y

only if Fx iff. Fy. No object y could have properties diverse from x and also be such that x = y. No account of "change" over time or across worlds can violate Leibniz's laws.
21 For further references to this phenomenon see Lewis 1979, 1986. Many thanks to Mark Johnston and Wolfgang Schwarz for valuable discussion of these points.
22 For similar arguments against self-explanation, see Mackie 1982, 84ff. For an interesting discussion of Mackie's objections see Garcia 1986, 479–488.
23 There are important exceptions. See Salmon 1989, 3–34.
24 Lewis offers one response to this objection in 1986, 123ff.
25 It is important to keep in mind that theistic modal realism is not a multiverse theory. On multiverse theories, God creates every on-balance good universe, but God creates only one possible world. On theistic modal realism, God creates every possible world.
26 I use "near" and "far" metaphorically here. The near worlds are the most similar worlds and the worlds farther away are the less similar worlds.
27 See Kraay 2018.
28 It is worth noting briefly that theistic modal realism also avoids any cost in libertarian freewill, indeterminate quantum effects, or modal imagination. The fact that everything in the pluriverse exists, occurs, and obtains necessarily is consistent with the existence of worlds w and w' that are exact duplicates until their divergence at a time t. It's possible that in w at t A occurs and in w' at t ~A occurs, or in w at t S does A and in w' at t S's counterpart does ~A. Indeterminism and libertarian freewill are consistent with the absolute explanation of the pluriverse. There is also no imaginable world—imagine, for instance, lawless worlds in which objects come into existence uncaused or completely random worlds in which there are not even statistical laws or worlds featuring both meticulous providence and significantly free moral agents who always do what's right—that is inconsistent with the absolute explanation of the pluriverse. Theistic modal realism offers unmatched theoretical advantages at extremely reasonable costs. The discovery that the pluriverse includes an Anselmian God should be particularly welcome news.

Bibliography

Adams, Robert M. (1974), "Theories of Actuality," *Noûs* 8 (3): 211–31.
Almeida, Michael. (2017a), "Theistic Modal Realism I: The Challenge of Theistic Actualism," *Philosophy Compass* 12: 1–14.

Almeida, Michael. (2017b), "Theistic Modal Realism II: Theoretical Benefits," *Philosophy Compass* 12: 1–17.

Bennett, Jonathan. (1984), *A Study of Spinoza's Ethics*. Indianapolis: Hackett.

Cameron, Ross P. (2009), "God Exists at Every (Modal Realist) World: Response to Sheehy," *Religious Studies* 45: 95–100.

Chalmers, David. (2002), "Does Conceivability Entails Possibility?" in *Conceivability and Possibility*, edited by Tamar Szabó Gendler and John Hawthorne, pp. 145–200. Oxford: Clarendon Press.

Deasy, Daniel. (2009), "The Moving Spotlight Theory," *Philosophical Studies* 172 (8): 2073–89.

Does God Matter?: Essays on the Axiological Consequences of Theism. (2018), Klaas Kraay (ed.). London: Routledge.

Earman, John. (1986), *A Primer on Determinism*. Dordrecht: D. Reidel Publishing.

Garcia, Laura. (1986), "Can the be a Self-Explanatory Being?" *Southern Journal of Philosophy* XXXIV (4): 479–88.

Griffin, Michael V. (2013), *Leibniz, God, and Necessity*. Cambridge: Cambridge University Press.

Leibniz, Gottfried. (1697) [1989], "On the Ultimate Origination of Things," in *G.W. Leibniz: Philosophical Essays*, edited by R. Ariew and D. Garber, pp. 149–54. Indianapolis: Hackett Publishing.

Leibniz, Gottfried. (1710) [1996], *Theodicy*. La Salle: Open Court Press.

Leibniz, Gottfried. (1714) [1973], "Monadology," in *Leibniz: Philosophical Writings*, edited by G. H. R. Parkinson, pp. 179–94. New Jersey: Rowman and Littlefield.

Leibniz, Gottfried. (1714) [1989], "Principles of Nature and Grace, Based on Reason," in *G.W. Leibniz: Philosophical Essays*, edited by R. Ariew and D. Garber, pp. 206–12. Indianapolis: Hackett Publishing.

Lewis, David. (1970), "Anselm and Actuality," *Noûs* 4 (2): 175–88.

Lewis, David. (1978), "Truth in Fiction," *American Philosophical Quarterly* 15 (1): 37–46.

Lewis, David. (1979), "Counterfactual Dependence and Time's Arrow," *Noûs* 13 (4): 455–76.

Lewis, David. (1983), *Philosophical Papers I*. Oxford: Oxford University Press.

Lewis, David. (1986), *On the Plurality of Worlds*. Oxford: Blackwell Publishers.

Lewis, David. (2001), *On the Plurality of Worlds*. Oxford: Oxford University Press.

Lewis, Stephanie. (2015), "Where (in Logical Space) Is God?" in *A Companion to David Lewis*, edited by Barry Loewer and Jonathan Schaffer, pp. 206–19. Malden: Wiley-Blackwell.

Mackie, John (1982), *The Miracle of Theism*. Oxford: Oxford University Press.

Maitzen, Stephen. (2013), "Questioning the Question," in *The Puzzle of Existence: Why Is There Something Rather than Nothing?*, edited by Tyron Goldschmidt, pp. 252–71. London: Routledge.

Morreall, John (1980), "God as Self-Explanatory," *The Philosophical Quarterly* 30 (120): 206–14.

Oppy, Graham. (2006), *Arguing About Gods*. Cambridge: Cambridge University Press.

Plantinga, Alvin. (1974), *The Nature of Necessity*. Oxford: Oxford University Press.

Salmon, Nathan. (1989), "The Logic of What Might Have Been," *The Philosophical Review* 98 (1): 3–34.

Skyrms, Bryan. (1976), "Possible Worlds, Physics and Metaphysics," *Philosophical Studies* 30 (5): 323–32.

Swinburne, Richard. (2004), *The Existence of God*, 2nd edn. Oxford: Oxford University Press.

van Inwagen, Peter. (1983), *An Essay on Free Will*. Oxford: Clarendon Press.

van Inwagen, Peter. (2009), *Metaphysics*, 3rd edn. Boulder: Westview.

Commentary on "On Discovering God in the Pluriverse"

Travis Dumsday

There is unfortunately not much I can contribute to the discussion of Almeida's very interesting chapter, insofar as he and I are operating from within exceedingly divergent metaphysical frameworks (e.g., on issues of modality, essence, identity, and the nature of the representation relationship). However, I do have a thought regarding the distinction he employs between permanentism and impermanentism. He writes:

> Permanentism is the temporal view that it is always the case that everything is always something. According to permanentism there is no time at which anything comes into, or goes out of, existence. Impermanentism is of course the negation of permanentism. It is the view that things sometimes come into and sometimes go out of existence. The theistic modal realist response to the problem of moral indifference is that the good and evil in the pluriverse exists necessarily, but it does not exist permanently. There is a total amount of good and evil in the pluriverse, but it is not true that there is a permanent amount of good and evil in the pluriverse. (33)

I am not entirely sure how much this observation would (if true) assist in upholding the positive axiological status of theistic modal realism and its accompanying necessarily existent pluriverse. It may be that it remains possible that the value of the pluriverse as a whole will rise over time (or perhaps *meta*-time, if we are measuring temporal progress across all possible worlds, some of which may have begun at a time while others may be infinitely old?). However, since Almeida's view is that all possible worlds exist, among those possible worlds will be a great many (infinitely many?) hellscape worlds. These are possible worlds in which all of the billions of conscious beings existing within them are born into undeserved states of unremitting agony and live a hundred years of intense suffering with no meaning or other countervailing goods (like a heavenly afterlife) attached to their lives. And the very nature of these hellscape worlds is that the suffering going on within them is everlasting—or perhaps in *some* of them it is everlasting (the world never ends and the suffering of its inhabitants never ends or lessens in any way) while in others it is temporary. Both are, after all, possible worlds. Thus, even if the value of the pluriverse as a whole might be impermanent, rising over time, clearly the rising waters fail to lift all boats. This seems problematic.

And I do not see a way out of affirming the presence of hellscape worlds within the pluriverse. If I have understood Almeida correctly, his system *requires* the reality of hellscape worlds. He writes, "Theistic modal realism takes as the object of God's creation *the totality of metaphysical reality*, all actualia and all possibilia. To the question, what did God create, the answer is *everything unrestrictedly*. Everything in the pluriverse—all of divine creation—is a vast concrete reality and it all exists in exactly the same way" (22). And among those possibilia are surely eternal hellscapes, pockets of permanent unjust torment of billions of conscious beings. Moreover, he explicitly moves away from any attempt to weaken the pluriverse view in favor of a multiverse ontology in which God only creates minimally decent universes. Thus, in footnote 25 he states, "It is important to keep in mind that theistic modal realism is not a multiverse theory. On multiverse theories, God creates every on balance good universe, but God creates only one possible world. On theistic modal realism, God creates every possible world" (38). Despite this, Almeida claims that theistic modal realism implies at least narrow impersonal pro-theism, on the ground that it is an objective good, in a certain respect, that God manifest His glory via the creative instantiation of all possibilities (27).

It is possible that I am misreading Almeida on one or another of these points, but if not then I worry that his position is vulnerable to something like the following axiological objection:

1. If theistic modal realism entails the reality of divinely created hellscape worlds, then theistic modal realism also entails the falsity of both wide and narrow impersonal pro-theism (because any resultant manifestation of divine glory would be nullified by the hellscapes).
2. Theistic modal realism entails the reality of divinely created hellscape worlds.
    Therefore,

3. Theistic modal realism also entails the falsity of both wide and narrow impersonal pro-theism (because any resultant manifestation of divine glory would be nullified by the hellscapes).

Commentary on "On Discovering God in the Pluriverse"

Perry Hendricks

In his chapter, Almeida explicates his version of theistic modal realism, and defends it against various objections. According to theistic modal realism, all possible worlds exist and God (of necessity) created them. Moreover, God, as a necessary being, exists (put loosely) in all the possible worlds, and provides an absolute explanation of everything. The difference between theistic modal realism and nontheistic modal realism (aside from the former entailing God exists) is the fact that theistic modal realism provides an absolute explanation of everything: God, a necessary being, is self-explained, and his creative act explains the existence of everything aside from himself. Hence, there are no brute facts. Everything has an explanation.

Almeida thinks that theistic modal realism shows that narrow impersonal pro-theism—the view that God's existence makes the world better *in some respect*—is true. He says:

> Discovering that there exists an Anselmian God in the pluriverse is good news in the narrow impersonal sense. The Anselmian pluriverse is the manifestation of the glory of the divine creator who creates in accordance with the principle of plenitude. Everything that could exist does exist. In the Anselmian pluriverse we have an absolute explanation for everything that exists, occurs, or obtains in the entire pluriverse without any loss in freedom or contingency. (35)

Almeida's reasoning for thinking that he has shown narrow impersonal pro-theism is not the fact that everything that could exist does exist, since this also happens on nontheistic modal realism. Instead, his reasoning appears to be just the fact that theistic modal realism provides us with an absolute explanation of everything while nontheistic modal realism does not. There is no doubt one sense in which Almeida is right here. Narrow impersonal pro-theism just says that God's existence makes the world better *in some respect*. And to discover that theistic modal realism is true, as opposed to nontheistic modal realism, means that the world is no doubt better *in some respect*. However, the "narrow" answers to the axiological question about God's existence (e.g., narrow impersonal pro-theism and narrow impersonal anti-theism) are *easy* to establish: it is *easy* to show that all narrow positions are true. For example, we can easily show that narrow impersonal anti-theism is true: if we discovered that theistic modal realism is true, then the world is worse in the sense that atheists have false beliefs. Hence, narrow impersonal anti-theism is true. This also suffices to establish narrow personal anti-theism, since the world will be worse *for* atheists, since *their* beliefs about atheism and God turn out to be false. Hence, narrow personal anti-theism is true. Simple arguments like this can be used to show that all narrow positions are true. But this is not an interesting result.

Perhaps, however, Almeida could expand his argument to show that *wide* impersonal pro-theism is true, or, at least, that discovering theistic modal realism is true would mean the world is *significantly* more valuable. The value would need to come from the fact that theistic modal realism provides an absolute explanation of everything, since this is the difference between theistic and nontheistic modal realism that Almeida is concerned with. But *why* does having an absolute explanation for everything make the world better? Why should we prefer a world in which there is an absolute explanation for everything to one in which there is no such explanation? It is not at all clear why we should. Indeed, it seems perfectly rational for one not to prefer a world in which there is an absolute explanation. For example, suppose that S is given a choice: she can exist in world W or world W*. Her life is the exact same in both worlds. The only difference is that W* has an absolute explanation of everything while W does not. Should S prefer W* to W? If her life is the same in both, the answer seems to be a clear "No." There is no reason for her to prefer W* to W since her life is the same in both cases. Her choice in living in W or W* is arbitrary. Or, if there is some reason for S to prefer W*, it is not at all clear what it is. While explanations are valuable in certain areas (for example, having an explanation of a disease may help one eliminate or prevent the disease), it is unclear why an *absolute* explanation *of everything* would be valuable. This is *not* to say that *God*, the source of absolute explanation, is not valuable. Rather, it is merely to say that an absolute explanation of everything is not valuable in itself—or, at least, it is not clear *why* it would be.

It might be tempting at this point to cite various goods that flow from having an absolute explanation. For example, one might suggest that if theistic modal realism is true, then God provides us with an absolute explanation for everything, and God would also ensure that there is a pleasant afterlife for (at least some) people. And this means that the world is better—or, at least, significantly improved—if God exists. While something like this line of reasoning may be right, it does not appear to be what Almeida has in mind: Almeida mentions only the fact that theistic modal realism gives an absolute explanation of everything, *not* that the source of absolute explanation (i.e., God) brings about other goods.[1] So, we must not look for goods that flow from having an absolute explanation, but must focus on the value of the absolute explanation itself.

In conclusion, while Almeida does a valiant job defending theistic modal realism against various objections to it, he does not provide us with a strong case for thinking that a significant version of pro-theism is true. While he is right in thinking that he has shown *narrow* impersonal pro-theism to be true, narrow answers to the axiological question are easy to come by. So, the reader is left wondering whether there may be an unstated reason for thinking that an absolute explanation of everything is valuable in a significant way. I invite Almeida to elaborate on this, and explain why having an absolute explanation of everything makes a world preferable to worlds in which there is no such explanation.

Note

1 True, Almeida says that theistic modal realism preserves contingency and freedom. But he does not argue that contingency and freedom are not had on nontheistic modal realism.

Commentary on "On Discovering God in the Pluriverse"

Graham Oppy

Mike Almeida endorses what he takes to be a theistic adaptation of David Lewis's modal realism. On Almeida's account, there is a vast concrete pluriverse created by an Anselmian maximal God who is present throughout the pluriverse. In his view, God and the pluriverse exist and are as they are of "absolutely unrestricted necessity." However, while God is "intrinsically necessary," everything else in the pluriverse is only "extrinsically necessary." In response to the objection that there is no contingency in the pluriverse, Almeida replies that "contingency arises in the pluriverse . . . from lowering the standards of representation," that is, "from the accommodation of assertions that presuppose less than perfectly strict standards of similarity in the selection of counterparts" (27). In response to the objection that Almeida's claim that the existence of God is self-explanatory should be rejected because it is impossible for anything to be self-explanatory, Almeida replies that (i) for any p, $\Box\Box p$ explains $\Box p$ and (ii) for any p, $\Box\Box p$ is identical to $\Box p$, whence it follows that $\Box p$ explains itself. In response to the observation that every instance of good and evil in the pluriverse exists of necessity, Almeida notes that it does not follow from this that every evil in the pluriverse exists permanently: "the total amount of good and evil in the pluriverse at t need not equal the total amount of good and evil in the universe at t'" (33). Almeida concludes that learning that there is an Anselmian maximal God in the pluriverse is good news, at least for some people in some respects.

Almeida's views provoke lots of questions. I can only consider some of them here, and then only in a very sketchy fashion.

1. Almeida's response to the objection that there is no contingency in the pluriverse conflates metaphysical and merely linguistic considerations. Sure, we can introduce linguistic conventions that allow us to talk *as if* there is contingency, but that doesn't make it the case that there *is* contingency. Given the framework that Almeida adopts, counterparts are not us: talk that supposes or pretends that they are cannot yield literal truth.

2. Almeida's response to the objection that nothing can be self-explanatory fails. (It is, I think, obvious that it must fail: after all, "A because A" is always an explanatory solecism. If I ask you "Why does God exist?" and you reply "Because God exists," I am bound to think either that you are not being straight with me or else that there is something wrong with your understanding of how explanation works.) I'm inclined to reject both of the claims that Almeida appeals to in his argument on behalf of self-explanation. I do not think that there is any p for which $\Box\Box p$ explains $\Box p$; rather, for any (non-modalized) p

for which it is true that □p, it is a brute fact—something that has no further explanation—that □p. To be necessarily true is to be true no matter what; but if something is true no matter what, then there isn't anything to which appeal can be made to explain why it is true. (In passing, I should note that, if this is right, then there is no distinction between intrinsic necessity and extrinsic necessity: there is just brute necessity.) Further—and perhaps more uncontroversially—it is not true that, for any p, □□p is identical to □p. Sure, it is true in S4 and S5 that ⊢ □□p ↔ □p. But there are weaker logics—for example, K and T—in which we do not have ⊢ □□p ↔ □p. And this is enough to establish that □□p and □p are distinct propositions.

3. Almeida's response to the problem of moral indifference assumes that there is a single time scale for the entire pluriverse. That assumption looks questionable, but suppose we accept it. Given Lewisian assumptions about plenitude and recombination, it seems that we have a straightforward argument that the balance of good over evil is not increasing over time in the pluriverse. At any time, there are worlds in the pluriverse where the balance of good over evil is whatever you please; and, at any time, there are no fewer worlds in which balance of good over evil is worsening than there are worlds in which the balance of good over evil is improving. If an arm breaks in a world at t and mends at t', then there are other worlds where counterpart arms are fine at t, get steadily more painful until t', and then break. (In this discussion, I ignore the obvious worries about how to measure the balance of good over evil across a large cardinality of worlds. If there were some way of measuring how much good and how much evil there is in the pluriverse, it is very hard to believe that this might vary over a finite time interval, and it is hardly any easier to believe that this might vary over the entire span of the pluriverse.)

4. There is an apparent tension between two things that Almeida says about the worlds of the pluriverse: (1) they are causally isolated individuals; and (2) God is the creator of all of the worlds of the pluriverse. However, exactly, we are meant to understand God's creation of the worlds, we are surely meant to think that it is causal. (How else can it explain the existence of the worlds?) But, if God's creation is causal, then all of the worlds of the pluriverse have a common cause. And, if all of the worlds of the pluriverse have a common cause, then they are not causally isolated. (Suppose, as some theists think, that there can be causal influence of creatures on God. Then, for all that Almeida

says, there could be causal chains that originate in one world and pass through God to another world.)

5. Almeida seems to say that the comparative value question should be taken to be *whether it is better to learn that God exists than to learn that God does not exist*, and not *whether it would be better to learn that God exists than to learn that God does not exist*. Almeida draws two distinctions: (a) between conditional and counterfactual formulations, and (b) between the epistemic and the metaphysical possibility that God exists. Almeida objects to counterfactual formulations because of the "logical and metaphysical obstacles" to assessing counter-possibles. Almeida suggests that, in conditional formulations, the relevant possibilities are ways the world *might actually be* rather than ways the world *might have been*. Moreover, he suggests that we might gloss these possibilities as possible for all we know *a priori*, or possible for all we know for certain, or possible for all we know, or possible for all we justifiably believe. It seems to me that, at best, there are two independent issues here. (Curiously, Almeida's own initial formulation of the epistemic question is counterfactual: "would it be better if we learned that our world includes a God then if we learned that our world does not include a God.") Furthermore, it seems to me that worries about counter-possibles press on conditionals in the same way that they press on counterfactuals: if I think that it is impossible that God exists—and hence impossible that I learn that God exists—then it is, at the very least, hard for me to evaluate the claim that it is better for God to exist than it is for God not to exist. Beyond this, it seems to me that, if called to assess the claim that it is better to learn that God exists than to learn that God does not exist, I ought—and ought want—to assess this relative to my entire worldview. I am not interested in restricting my attention to what I know *a priori*, or what I know, or what I'm certain of, or what I justifiably believe—even if I have some way of hiving these off from what I believe. Rather, I'm quite happy to say that, since I would only learn that God exists if God exists, and yet it is impossible that God exists, there is no way that I can coherently endorse the claim that it is better to learn that God exists than it is to learn that God does not exist.

6. After observing that Lewis himself was an unwavering atheist and a polytheist, Almeida notes that Lewis's views on the nature of the pluriverse are not the last word, and then launches into his description of theistic modal

realism. But those sympathetic to naturalism ought to note a different tack: Lewis himself would have done better to say that there are no gods anywhere in the pluriverse. (Here, I agree with Steffi Lewis, who made this point in a talk that she gave at an AAP conference.) I myself favor a much more restrictive view of what is possible, taking the laws and some initial part of actuality to be necessary, and allowing that such departures from actuality as there are result solely from different outcomes of indeterministic causes.

Reply to Commentaries on "On Discovering God in the Pluriverse"

Michael Almeida

1 Reply to Dumsday

Travis Dumsday raises a very interesting objection concerning the overall value of the modal realist's pluriverse.

> However, since Almeida's view is that all possible worlds exist, among those possible worlds will be a great many (infinitely many?) hellscape worlds. These are possible worlds in which all of the billions of conscious beings existing within them are born into undeserved states of unremitting agony and live a hundred years of intense suffering with no meaning or other countervailing goods (like a heavenly afterlife) attached to their lives. And the very nature of these hellscape worlds is that the suffering going on within them is everlasting—or perhaps in *some* of them it is everlasting (the world never ends and the suffering of its inhabitants never ends or lessens in any way) while in others it is temporary. Both are, after all, possible worlds. (41)

Klaas Kraay has raised a similar objection to theistic modal realism on at least two occasions (Kraay 2011, 2018). Concerning the formulation of the objection above, note that it's everyone's view that all possible worlds exist—Plantingan actualists, Ludovician modal realists, Stalnaker actualists, and so on. This is not a view unique to modal realists. It is everyone's view that all possible worlds exist since possible worlds necessarily exist.[1] Dumsday is not worried that every world exists. He is worried that every (modal realist) world is *concrete*. The sentient inhabitants of possible worlds are creatures ontologically no different from you and I. Possible worlds are not abstract descriptions of ways things might have been, but concrete ways things in fact are in other regions of the vast pluriverse. Some of the ways things are in other concrete regions include, on Dumsday's reckoning, hellscape worlds: possible worlds in which billions of sentient beings endure undeserved and unremitting agony and intense suffering, living meaningless lives with no other countervailing goods such as a heavenly afterlife. The suffering in those worlds is no different in kind from the suffering in our world. It is a terrible fact that there are such worlds, if in fact there are such worlds.

But is there any reason to believe Dumsday's modal assertion about the existence of such possible worlds? Anselmians like Tom Morris are much less confident that there are such worlds. Morris in fact flatly rejects the notion that worlds of that sort are possible.[2] Morris recognizes that if there are such hellscape worlds then—on any modal metaphysics you please—there is a powerful argument that God does not exist. On any view of the nature of possible worlds, the very possibility of the worlds Dumsday describes generates the modal problem of evil.[3] Dumsday's hellscape problem is not unique to theistic modal realism. It's everybody's problem.[4]

But let's suppose there exist hellscape worlds as Dumsday suggests. Do such worlds present a problem of evil for theistic modal realism? It is one of the major advantages of theistic modal realism that every intrinsically evil state of affairs in every possible world is *necessary to the greatest total good*. The total amount of good in the pluriverse is the greatest amount of good possible. It is impossible to bring about the greatest total good without bringing about the sorts of worlds that Dumsday describes, assuming those worlds are genuinely possible. There are no alternative pluriverses that include only on balance good worlds. There is in fact a single pluriverse that includes the greatest amount of total good.

The worlds that Dumsday describes are not only necessary to the realization of all possible good; they are themselves extrinsically necessary objects. The pluriverse is necessary and everything in the pluriverse exists necessarily, including the worst worlds. Spinoza describes a very similar view in the *Ethics*:

> Things could not have been produced by God in any other way or in any other order than is the case. (E1p33pr)

If the pluriverse is necessarily as it is, then hellscape worlds are necessarily existing objects. It is impossible that there should not have been hellscape worlds, if in fact there are such worlds. The existence of such worlds presents no moral problem for God since God could have done nothing to prevent hellscape worlds from existing.

But what of Dumsday's objection that hellscape worlds present a problem for the claim that theistic modal realism offers a narrow impersonal advantage for theism?

> If theistic modal realism entails the reality of divinely created hellscape worlds, then theistic modal realism also entails the falsity of both wide and narrow impersonal pro-theism (because any resultant manifestation of divine glory would be nullified by the hellscapes). (42)

First note that theistic modal realism entails the existence of hellscape worlds if and only if Plantingan or Stalnaker actualism entails hellscape worlds. If such worlds exist, then they necessarily exist and so exist no matter what metaphysical commitments one takes on. Second note that "On Discovering God in the Pluriverse" does not aim to show that the manifestation of God's glory in creation entails wide or narrow pro-theism. The goal of "On Discovering God in the Pluriverse" was to show that theistic modal realism offers *theoretical advantages* unavailable to alternative nontheistic and theistic positions. Those theoretical advantages are what justify the narrow impersonal pro-theistic position.

2 Reply to Hendricks

Perry Hendricks's main objection is that establishing a narrow impersonal pro-theistic position is easy, and so there is no genuine achievement in "On Discovering God in the Pluriverse":

> Almeida . . . does not provide us with a strong case for thinking that a significant version of pro-theism is true. While he is right in thinking that he has shown *narrow* impersonal pro-theism to be true, narrow answers to the axiological question are easy to come by. So, the reader is left wondering whether there may be an unstated reason for thinking that an absolute explanation of everything is valuable in a significant way. (45)

The form of reasoning here is interesting. Why not apply the same reasoning to Kandinsky's *Composition VIII*? The work is no big deal, we should conclude on this line of criticism, since anyone can draw lines on canvas. But, of course, there's drawing lines on canvas and then there's drawing lines on canvas. The same goes for narrow impersonal pro-theism. Not every version of narrow impersonal pro-theism is equal in significance, value, and achievement to every other version.

What is shown in "On Discovering God in the Pluriverse" is that theistic modal realism offers theoretical advantages unavailable to alternative positions. Nothing in the chapter aims to show—or even to consider—questions about the practical value of theistic modal realism. The overall well-being of the inhabitants of the pluriverse is one way, but obviously not the only way, to measure the value of theistic and nontheistic worlds.

What exactly are the theoretical advantages that constitute the value of theistic modal realism? Why is the view narrowly pro-theist? There isn't space to describe in detail all of the theoretical advantages of the view, but I can provide a partial list.[5] (i) Theistic modal realism provides an absolute explanation for *everything*. It explains all actualia and all possibilia. On theistic modal realism the entire pluriverse is fully intelligible. (ii) There are no brute facts in the pluriverse and there is no loss of contingency. (iii) Theistic modal realism avoids moral indifference and (iv) permits indeterministic worlds. (v) No account of the nature of metaphysical reality provides a better reconciliation of libertarian freedom and meticulous providence. (vi) It offers a solution to *every* problem of evil since there are no non-necessary instances of evil in the pluriverse. (vii) Theistic modal realism satisfies the principle of plenitude—A. O. Lovejoy's famous principle—and provides a proper object of divine creation.[6] The object of creation is unsurpassable in magnitude and goodness. (viii) The view offers a solution to the problem of No-Best World and to the problem of our Less-than-Best world. (ix) To list one last advantage, it offers an explanation for the apparent arbitrariness of the actual world. It explains why we have these particular laws and constants and not some others, for instance. These and many other theoretical advantages I do not have the space to list constitute the reasons why discovering that we inhabit an Anselmian pluriverse would be very good news.

3 Reply to Oppy

Graham Oppy offers a series of incisive and targeted objections to my chapter, "On Discovering God in the Pluriverse." While all of the objections are interesting, I will have to focus on the most problematic ones. In my discussion of contingency, Oppy initially worries that I have conflated metaphysics and linguistics. On my characterization, theistic modal realism is committed to both counterpart theory and modal contextualism, and it can appear that neither one has much to do with questions about modality. Everyone agrees that it is possible that Smith is left-handed just if some representative of Smith somewhere in metaphysical space is left-handed. Who or what are our representatives? We get either descriptions of our representatives in each world (i.e., sets of sentences or propositions or states of affairs describing our representatives) or concrete—most often flesh and blood—representatives. In either case, what is possible, contingent, or necessary requires the existence of representatives in possible worlds. And what is possible or contingent or necessary for you—again, whether you're an actualist or modal realist or whatnot—depends on what representatives are invoked. Can I speak Finnish? The answer to that depends on which representatives you're invoking in context. Yes, I have the right vocal apparatus. No, I was never trained. Can I play a concerto? Again, it depends on the representatives you have in mind. No, I've never learned to play piano. Yes, I have all of the physical requirements. Every view invokes varying representatives to answer such modal questions, not just theistic modal realism. The context determines which representatives matter to answering yes or no to your modal question. We indicate in context what makes one representative or another relevant to answering the question. Sometimes the only representative that matters is you yourself. Can you here, now, keeping everything as it is, high jump 7 feet? The answer to that modal question depends on what you will do, since you alone are your only representative in this context. It is not linguistics; it is the way modal metaphysics works for everyone. Our only disagreement is over what counts as a representative: some description of a way you might be or some object that is a way you might be.

Oppy finds the concept of self-explanation incoherent, indeed obviously so:

> If I ask you "Why does God exist?" and you reply "Because God exists," I am bound to think either that you are not being straight with me, or else that there is something wrong with your understanding of how explanation works. (46)

It is true that terms like "self-explanation" or worse, "self-caused," invite confusion and misunderstanding. And I agree that the explanation for God's existence cannot credibly be that God exists. But of course I never say that the explanation for God's existence is that God exists. I say that the explanation for God's existence is that God has the *de re* property of necessarily existing, or $(\exists y)(God = y)$ if and only if $\Box(\exists y)(God = y)$. That is, in Steven Maitzen's terms, I offer the strongest possible explanation for God's existence: "the fact that N had to obtain, occur, or exist—is one explanation, maybe the strongest possible explanation, for why N does obtain, occur, or exist" (Maitzen 2013, 256). But of course the explanation doesn't end there. It is also true that $\Box(\exists y)(God = y)$ if and only if $\Box\Box(\exists y)(God = y)$. So, we have the fact that $\Box\Box(\exists y)(God = y)$ explaining the fact that $\Box(\exists y)(God = y)$ and so on upward, for every iteration of $\Box$. And since it is true in any logic as strong as S4 that $\vdash \Box(\Box\Box(\exists y)(God = y) \longleftrightarrow \Box(\exists y)(God = y))$, we know that the proposition on the left side of that biconditional is identical to the proposition on the right side of that biconditional. The right conclusion is that necessarily existing objects explain their own existence.

But maybe the worry is that this is not genuine self-explanation. What we in fact have initially is a *de re* property, $\Box Fg$, of an object g—indeed we have a haecceity of g—explaining another property, Fg, of object g. No doubt the properties involved in the initial explanation are distinct properties. The explanans is $\Box Fg$ and the explanandum is Fg, and the explanation is that $\Box(\Box Fg \longrightarrow Fg)$. The explanation for g does not involve any object other than g and the properties of g. So self-explanation involves a distinct explanans and explanandum—two different properties—but a single object.[7] God's essential properties explain God's existence.

Oppy objects further to my claim that we can consistently hold that all of the evil in the pluriverse exists necessarily and we can reduce the total amount of evil in the pluriverse.

> Almeida's response to the problem of moral indifference assumes that there is a single time scale for the entire pluriverse. That assumption looks questionable, but suppose we accept it. Given Lewisian assumptions about plenitude and recombination, it seems that we have a straightforward argument that the balance of good over evil is not increasing over time in the pluriverse. At any time, there are worlds in the pluriverse where the balance of good over evil is whatever you please; and, at any time, there are no fewer worlds in which balance of good over evil is worsening than there are worlds in which the balance of good over evil is improving. (47)

In "On Discovering God in the Pluriverse," I argue that the proposition <necessarily p> does not entail <permanently p> and so does not entail <necessarily permanently p>. The fact that it is necessarily true that Jones suffers does not entail that Jones's suffering is permanent or that Jones's suffering is ineliminable. It is in general a mistake to think that necessarily existing objects, events, states of affairs never cease to exist, occur, or obtain. The easiest way to see the difference between necessarily existing objects and permanently existing objects is to imagine that our world is a "dead end" world or a Spinozistic world. If so, then relative to our world, no other world is possible. It is probably easiest of all just to imagine that our world is the only possible world. If our world is in fact the only possible world, as Spinoza seems to have thought, then everything existing in our world necessarily exists. You and I, for instance, necessarily exist, since we exist in every possible world, namely, the actual world. But you and I obviously do not permanently exist. The bad news is that we will both, alas, go out of existence. The good news is that actual evil isn't permanent, either. There is a total amount of evil in the world and every single instance of evil necessarily exists. But it does not follow that all actual evil permanently exists. It doesn't. We can eliminate evil and reduce the total amount of evil in the world and in the pluriverse.

The very same reasoning that we applied to Spinozistic worlds applies to the theistic pluriverse. The total amount of evil in the pluriverse is reducible and in fact is fluctuating. It is perfectly possible that, as of this very moment (central standard time, actual world), the total amount of evil in the pluriverse approximates zero, since it is possible that at this moment the total evil in all other worlds has gone out of existence. But the central point of distinguishing necessity and permanence is to underscore the fact that we can reduce the total amount of evil in the pluriverse, contrary to a common objection to the metaphysics of modal realism.

Notes

1 But see Adams (1981) for the view that possible worlds are contingent objects whose existence depends on contingently existing singular proposition.
2 See Morris 1985.
3 See Guleserian 1983.

4 Multiverse theorists do attempt to avoid the modal problem of evil, but their account of divine creation is simply incoherent. See Almeida 2017a.
5 For a detailed discussion of the advantages see Almeida 2017b.
6 See Lovejoy 1932:

> I shall call it the principle of plenitude but shall use the term to cover ... the thesis ... that no genuine potentiality of being can remain unfulfilled, that the extent and the abundance of the creation must be as great as the possibility of existence and commensurate with the productive capacity of a "perfect" and inexhaustible Source, and that the world is the better the more things it contains.

For fascinating discussion of the history of the principle of plenitude, see Knuuttila 1980.

7 All additional explanations—$\Box\Box\Box Fg$ for $\Box Fg$, $\Box\Box\Box Fg$ for $\Box\Box Fg$, and so on—add no new properties or objects. The explanation $\Box(\Box Fg \longrightarrow Fg)$ in the case under discussion is $\Box(\Box(\exists y)(God = y) \longrightarrow (\exists y)(God = y))$.

Bibliography

Adams, Robert M. (1981), "Actualism and Thisness," *Synthese* 49 (1): 3–41.

Almeida, Michael. (2017a), "The Multiverse and Divine Creation," *Religions* 8 (12): 258–69.

Almeida, Michael. (2017b), "Theistic Modal Realism II: Theoretical Benefits," *Philosophy Compass* 12 (7): 1–17.

Guleserian, Theodore. (1983), "God and Possible Worlds: The Modal Problem of Evil," *Noûs* 17 (2): 221–38.

Knuuttila, Simo, ed. (1980), *Reforging the Great Chain of Being*. Dordrecht-Holland: D. Reidel Publishing.

Kraay, Klaas. (2011), "Theism and Modal Collapse," *American Philosophical Quarterly* 48 (4): 361–72.

Kraay, Klaas. (2018), "One Philosopher's Bug Can Be Another's Feature: Reply to Almeida's 'Multiverse and Divine Creation,'" *Religions* 9 (1): 23: 1–9.

Lovejoy, A. O. (1932), *The Great Chain of Being*. Cambridge: Harvard University Press.

Maitzen, Stephen. (2013), "Questioning the Question," in *The Puzzle of Existence: Why Is There Something Rather than Nothing?*, edited by Tyron Goldschmidt, pp. 352–271 London: Routledge.

Morris, Thomas V. (1985), "The Necessity of God's Goodness," *New Scholasticism* 59 (4): 418–48. Reprinted in his (1987), *Anselmian Explorations*. Notre Dame: University of Notre Dame Press.

Spinoza, Benedict de. (2005), *Ethics*. London: Penguin Classics.

3

The Axiology of Theism

Expanding the Contrast Classes

Travis Dumsday

1 Introduction

Within the literature on the axiology of theism, two incompatible propositions are usually put in focus: the proposition that God exists and the proposition that metaphysical naturalism is true. Thus in considering whether the value of the world as a whole (and/or the value of certain aspects of the world) and the well-being of humanity (and/or the well-being of some persons considered individually) would be enhanced or diminished by the existence of God, theism is typically contrasted with a view according to which reality is exhausted by the physical—that is, according to which there are no divinities or souls or other irreducibly real immaterial entities. The focus on these two doctrines is unsurprising, given that theism (understood along broadly classical lines[1]) and metaphysical naturalism are the two most widely defended worldviews in contemporary analytic philosophy of religion.[2] However, alternative forms of theism (well-represented historically in the world's religious traditions) also warrant careful consideration in this context. Such alternatives are receiving increased attention within our subdiscipline more generally,[3] and such attention should be extended to the axiological debate. With that in mind, my aim in this chapter is to expand the relevant contrast classes by discussing possible axiological implications of two alternative forms of theism: pantheism and polytheism.

My goals here are modest. My aim is not to provide a set of deductive proofs, but rather a (hopefully) plausible lay of the land on which other interested parties can build. This will involve formulating assessments of the axiological status of the two views, *but these assessments will be tentative*. Moreover, they will be manifestly incomplete, on at least three fronts. First, pantheism and polytheism both admit of a variety of different formulations and have in fact appeared in importantly different versions. I cannot discuss all of these different versions, such that a narrowed focus is in each case required; this is likely to disappoint some, who will perhaps have a preference for an alternative left out of the discussion. Given space constraints (and unfortunate deficiencies in my own knowledge of world religions) this is unavoidable, and I must simply beg the indulgence of the reader. Second, there are obviously still other forms of theism (e.g., panentheism[4]) and also forms of nontheistic non-naturalism (e.g., animism,[5] panpsychism,[6] or J. L. Schellenberg's ultimism[7]) that might have been productively considered. In restricting my focus to pantheism and polytheism I do not intend to imply in any way that other such views are unworthy of reflection in this context. Third, again to keep the inquiry manageable I will contrast each of those two positions only with metaphysical naturalism. That is, in inquiring as to the axiological status of polytheism (say), the assumption will be that a polytheistic world is being compared with a world in which there are no gods or other irreducible spiritual entities at all. Polytheism will *not* be directly compared with a world in which there is only one God (i.e., the God of classical theism), or with worlds in which panentheism or pantheism or panpsychism (etc.) obtain. Trying to assess the relative axiological ranking of each of these non-naturalist positions relative to all the others would constitute a book project. Still, the inquiry conducted here could in principle provide ingredients for wider comparisons—that is, if it were judged that a polytheist world would be worse overall than a naturalist world, whereas a pantheist world would be better overall than a naturalist world, it would follow that a pantheist world would be better than a polytheist world, at least as contrasted with naturalism.

The remainder is divided up as follows: in the next section I provide a brief review of conceptual distinctions important for any discussion of the axiology of religion. These will already be familiar to the reader but are worth recalling insofar as they will be repeatedly employed in the subsequent discussion. The succeeding sections then cover the two alternative theisms. The method in those sections will be first to lay out in detail the specific version of the view that will be discussed, and then to consider its axiological status vis-à-vis metaphysical naturalism.

2 Conceptual Groundwork

Developing earlier work by Kahane (2011) and Kraay and Dragos (2013), Kraay (2018) identifies five basic positions concerning the axiology of theism: *pro-theism, anti-theism, neutralism, agnosticism,* and *quietism*. Roughly stated, a pro-theist maintains that, all else being equal,[8] it would be *better* that God exist than that He not exist; an anti-theist maintains that, all else being equal, it would be *worse* that God exist than that He not exist; a neutralist claims that a world in which God exists would be neither better nor worse than one in which He does not; an agnostic holds that the question is in principle answerable, but that in practice one should withhold judgment about it; and a quietist maintains that the question is in principle unanswerable. These five positions can then be further subdivided into *wide* versus *narrow* versions, and also *personal* versus *impersonal* versions. For instance, a *wide* pro-theist claims that it would be a better thing for the world considered overall that God exist, while a *narrow* pro-theist maintains that it would be a better thing in certain respects. Relatedly, an *impersonal* pro-theist claims that God's existence would render things better for anyone and everyone, while a *personal* pro-theist claims that the reality of God would be better for herself or for certain specific people.

These positions are formulated in comparative terms; that is, most of the current literature on the axiology of theism takes these positions to be assessments of *relative value*. An anti-theist claims that, all else being equal, a world without God would be a better world than one with God (overall or in some respects/for all or for some), but she is not thereby making the stronger claim that a world in which God exists would ipso facto be a *bad* world. It might actually be a good world, yet one whose value is still diminished in some way by God's presence.[9]

The various distinctions just made open up the possibility for a rather large array of views based on different combinations. For example, one might advocate *wide impersonal anti-theism* (WIAT), according to which God's existence would render the world worse overall and would diminish the well-being of every person; or one might plug for *narrow impersonal anti-theism* (NIAT), on which the truth of theism would be bad news in certain respects and for everyone but not necessarily bad news for reality considered overall (i.e., theism might still be a comparative good for the world as a whole, or at least might have a neutral impact on its value); or one might advocate *narrow personal neutralism* (NPN), according to which God's reality has neutral value implications in certain respects for certain specific persons (though perhaps not for everyone nor for reality considered overall).

Of course, still further divisions might be introduced if one were also to specify how these views combine with theism, atheism, or agnosticism. For instance, one might believe that God exists but think that in a certain respect this is a terrible thing for some (but not all) people, resulting in *theistic narrow personal anti-theism* (THINPAT). Or one might be an agnostic about the truth of theism while also thinking that the reality of God would be a wonderful thing for everyone and for reality considered overall, resulting in *agnostic wide impersonal pro-theism* (AWIPT). More complex, paired combinations of views are also available, as Kraay and Dragos point out: "For example, consider an atheist who thinks that God's existence would make things worse for her in certain respects, but who is unsure about the overall axiological import of theism. Such an atheist would be both a *narrow personal anti-theist* and a *wide impersonal agnostic*" (2013, 175).

So far not many of these conceptually possible views have actually found advocates in the literature; moreover theists have tended to advocate versions of pro-theism while atheists have generally gone in for versions of anti-theism (with some notable exceptions).[10] As this body of literature further develops, it will be interesting to see whether more of these possible positions are taken up as plausible options for belief.

To a considerable degree the preceding conceptual groundwork can be carried over into the alternative theisms taken up below. With respect to polytheism one can distinguish pro-polytheist, anti-polytheist, neutralist, agnostic, and quietist options, with the same wide/narrow and impersonal/personal subdivisions applying in each case. Pantheism, however, introduces some interesting complications with respect to those subdivisions, as we shall see shortly.

3 Pantheism

There are many different understandings of what exactly pantheism consists in. Here are some initial characterizations:

- Hedley distinguishes between "crude pantheism" and "subtle pantheism," taking the latter to be the formulation of real philosophical interest: "CP

= the belief that the entire cosmos just is, i.e. is strictly identical with, the divine: 'pan' is 'theos'. And SP = the belief in a higher unifying force which is both impersonal and immanent within the cosmos" (1996, 62).
- Sprigge presents his own initial formulation as follows: "So pantheism, in the sense in which I am taking it, identifies God and the Universe. We can take this specification a little further . . . if we say that, for the pantheist, 'God is the unified totality of all things.' This avoids the charge that pantheism consist merely in a cognitively vacuous renaming of the universe by a differently emotive word, for not everyone agrees that the universe is unified, in any sense likely to be intended; indeed some hold that there is really no such thing as the universe, just lots and lots of things" (1997, 191–92). He goes on to describe eleven different versions of pantheism, each of which accords with that basic definition (while still differing from one another in important respects), and each of which has had proponents in the history of philosophy.
- Steinhart writes that "[a] *pantheist* claims that (1) all existing things are unified; and (2) the maximally-inclusive unity is divine" (2004, 63).[11]

Brian Leftow in distinguishing between non-naturalist and naturalist forms of pantheism, first notes that identity claims sometimes have an eliminativist connotation. He writes, "When we identify temperature with mean molecular kinetic energy, we mean that only mmke, as we'd understood it, is really there. One extreme way God / universe identity can go is to 'eliminate' the universe: thus in advaita Vedanta, Brahman = the universe, and the consequence is taken to be that there is really just one, simple, immutable, atemporal, spiritual thing" (2016, 65–66). He then observes that at the opposite end of the spectrum are pantheists who posit that the physical cosmos is all that really exists but argues that one can still properly label it divine.

That should suffice to illustrate the diversity of understandings of "pantheism"—or, depending on one's perspective, the diversity of *types* of pantheism. Given this diversity, no assessment of the axiological status of pantheism would be possible without first specifying the understanding or version being employed. Thankfully, the present terms of discussion do at least circumscribe the options. First, in the Introduction I described pantheism as an alternative form of theism, and I contrasted it with metaphysical naturalism. As such versions of pantheism properly labeled as atheist or naturalist would not fit into this project, and can be left to one side, whatever their independent merits (about which I make no judgment here). Second, given the current terms of discussion it makes sense to work with a version of pantheism that is clearly distinct from the alternative theisms with which it is contrasted here, and also distinct from versions of nontheistic non-naturalism with which it is sometimes associated. This too limits the space of options, since certain versions of pantheism can properly be cross-classified as versions of panpsychism while others seem to blur the borderline between pantheism and panentheism.[12] With that in mind, the choice of a version of pantheism that is unambiguously pantheistic *and nothing but* becomes necessary (though again, that choice is determined by the structure of the project and should not be seen as indicating a preference on my own part). Third, by way of making the present discussion more obviously relevant as philosophy *of religion*, it would be an advantage if the version of pantheism taken up here were one that actually had representation within a major world religion.

Taking those three desiderata into account, the pantheism that will be considered here is the fifth version laid out by Sprigge, formulated as follows:

> The natural world and the multiplicity of conscious beings is an illusion, or at least a mere presentation, given to itself by a single Absolute which may be called "God" or at least plays something of the role of God for this point of view. Salvation consists in consciously realizing one's identity with this Absolute. The world of daily life, both physical nature and all its conscious inhabitants, are an illusion which one ultimate spiritual reality gives itself. Our salvation consists in our grasping the illusory nature of our world and of our separate existence and experiencing our identity with the One from which we were never really separate. This is the position of Advaita Vedanta as elaborated by Sankara. It is also the view of Erwin Schrodinger and in effect that of the almost forgotten, but highly interesting, Christian evolutionary pantheist Allanson Picton. (1997, 194)[13]

This version of pantheism, represented by a major school of Hindu thought, is itself open to multiple interpretations on several fronts.[14] Such further interpretive issues must unfortunately be left aside here. However, I will also assume (in keeping with the standard interpretation of Advaita Vedanta doctrine) that the Absolute is to be conceived as *nonpersonal*—that it cannot literally be ascribed personhood, insofar as it exceeds our finite conceptual distinctions between the personal and the impersonal.

Preliminaries having been completed, we can now inquire into the axiological implications of this version of pantheism: Should one favor pro-pantheism, anti-pantheism, neutralism, agnosticism, or quietism?

The first point that should be noted is that the application of the *wide/narrow* and *impersonal/personal* subdivisions becomes awkward here. If there is some deep, underlying identity between every finite object and the Absolute (and, by transitivity, every finite object with every other finite object) then it is not clear whether or to what extent a meaningful or significant distinction remains between reality as a whole and any particular aspect or mode of reality, or between the well-being of any person and all persons.

Yet that very complication may carry axiological import; if, for instance, I am awed by the vast grandeur of our galaxy, and (plausibly) interpret that response as indicative of some objective value possessed by our galaxy, then the fact that I am in some sense identical with the galaxy may mean that my own value status is thereby heightened. The fact that the galaxy in turn is in some sense identical with God by extension may lend both it and me a still more exalted value status—presumably an *infinite* value status.

On the other hand, I might reflect on the fact that in comparison with Reality itself I am merely an illusion, such that it would be a good thing for the world overall (and for me?) were I finally to realize this illusion and thus rid the world of my (strictly illusory) identity. And these two value assessments, different though they seem, may in turn be really equivalent, the same state of affairs regarded from two different angles. Or as Sprigge describes it, each perspective "in its own way levels all things either up or down to the same value, up if the world is seen as through and through equally divine, down if the world is seen as an illusion to be transcended in our quest for unity with the undifferentiated *One* of Sankara's vision" (1997, 202).

Given those potential complications, let's leave aside for the present the *wide/narrow* and *impersonal/personal* subdivisions as potentially inapplicable, and ask simply: On this conception of pantheism, is pro-pantheism true? That is, all else being equal, is it better that our world be a pantheist world, or worse? (Keep in mind that the direct contrast class is one in which the world is outwardly much the same, but metaphysical naturalism holds true.) The answer largely depends on the further question of whether the underlying Absolute Reality is to be regarded as intrinsically valuable, and if so, whether it is to be regarded as more intrinsically valuable than reality as a whole conceived along naturalist lines. And one might assume that the answer to that question would be immediately apparent: after all, if the Absolute is labeled "God," and "God" is in turn understood as a value-laden term indicating, minimally, something that is worthy of worship and absolute devotion,[15] then of course the Absolute is immensely (probably infinitely) valuable. Moreover, that is a kind or degree of value that plausibly would be absent from a naturalist world; the latter might instantiate some value—indeed perhaps *any* existing thing instantiates some value simply by virtue of existing[16]—but not the right kind or amount to render it an appropriate object of religious commitment.

Such an assessment would be too quick though, for at least three reasons. First, consider a scenario in which being is ipso facto valuable. In that case, a naturalist universe that happened to contain an infinite number of beings (perhaps due to a gunky ontology of material composition, or perhaps due to an infinite spatial extension combined with a substantivalist ontology of spatial regions, or due to an infinite past combined with a growing block ontology of time) would appear to instantiate an infinite quantity of value. Now, perhaps that would not make it equivalent in value to a pantheist world; maybe the value of the Absolute is somehow of a higher-order infinity, or maybe its value is of a different and incommensurable kind, such that the very attempt to make a comparison is misconceived.[17] But if one's initial justification for pro-pantheism is simply the idea that a pantheist world would be infinitely valuable (because divine) whereas a naturalist world would not be, then that justification seems to require further refinement.[18] Certainly, more work would be needed to show that the divine status of the Absolute automatically entails pro-pantheism vis-à-vis metaphysical naturalism, rather than, say, neutralism.

Second, the idea that intrinsic value can be literally attributed to the Absolute would in fact be a controversial claim. It is well known that advocates of the sort of pantheism under discussion here have historically displayed a tendency toward a radical apophaticism; thus thinkers within the Advaita Vedanta tradition have commonly claimed that the Absolute exceeds all our conceptual categories, such that none of our predicates—including our normative predicates—can be applied to it literally. As such, one might claim that the value status of a pantheist world vis-à-vis a naturalist world is simply inscrutable for us at present, thereby providing a justification for agnosticism rather than pro-pantheism.[19] Now, this line of thought might be resisted by reference to Hindu religious practice. Philosophically inclined practitioners of Hinduism accept this version of pantheism and yet still view worship of the Absolute as appropriate, indicating that they view it as immensely valuable, even while strictly denying the literal truth of value predicates as applied to it. That is true, but one wonders then whether the practice rationally coheres with the doctrine. One might opt to abandon the apophaticism, which is arguably not an essential feature of the view (at least as Sprigge has laid it out). But then the prior concern (and perhaps also the next) may become more acute.

Third, one might question the kind or degree of intrinsic value of the Absolute by reference to the moral and natural evil we witness in our world. The Absolute is of course not subject to censure on account of these evils (unlike the God of classical theism, it cannot be accused of knowingly allowing such evils), but we might still point to them as evidence that the Absolute is far from infinitely valuable. After all, if the illusions/manifestations/participations are like *this*, can we be so confident that the underlying Reality which they are expressing is of unsurpassable value, or even much value at all? Some pantheists openly acknowledge and apparently embrace the attribution of evils to the Absolute. Levine writes of pantheism in general, but in a way I think applicable to the particular version under discussion here:

> Pantheism does not claim that its divine Unity is a "perfect being" or benign at all (generally), or that it is omniscient etc. . . . It might be supposed that the existence of evil is inconsistent or incongruous with the "divinity" of the Unity. But this would have to be argued. In theism it is assumed that what is divine cannot also be (in part) evil. But why assume this is the case with pantheism? Even in Otto's account of the "holy" the holy has a demonic aspect. There seems little reason to suppose that what is divine cannot also, in part, be evil. At any rate, there is little reason for the pantheist to argue that what is divine can also be evil, since they can deny that evil falls within the purview of the divine Unity. To say that everything that exists constitutes a divine Unity (i.e., pantheism's essential claim) need not be interpreted in such a way so that it entails that all parts and every aspect of the Unity is divine or good. There can be a Unity and it can be divine without everything about it always, or even sometimes, being divine. (2007, section 9)

This perspective on the nature of the pantheistic God complicates the axiological debate still further. Yet it is a perspective that accords both with the philosophical doctrine espoused within Advaita Vedanta and with Hindu devotional practices. (E.g., the worship of gods and goddesses—here understood as finite personifications of the Absolute, interpreted either as literal beings or simply as symbols of the divine—that seem prima facie to be of morally questionable status, such as the blood-drenched Kali.) In an odd way, this may make the evil present in a pantheist world even more troubling than the evil present in a naturalist world; in the latter, evil mars the overall value of the world (perhaps enough to make it a bad world overall, perhaps not), but at least much of this evil has the virtue of random purposelessness. Pain and fear and death and betrayal and all the horrors of natural and human history are simply *there*, and there isn't much more to be said. By contrast, whatever evil is present in a pantheist world would be rooted in and reflective of some deeper Reality, one into which our identities will ultimately be absorbed. The latter model may be seen by some as disturbing, in particular if the evils of our world are viewed as especially grave.[20] That having been said, it needs to be stressed that Levine's talk of the "demonic" aspect of the holy is obviously intended as metaphorical; the Absolute is nonpersonal and so, as noted above, cannot literally be seen as wicked, if wickedness is understood in terms of conscious and deliberate choice of evil. Yet to the extent that conscious and deliberate evils are found in our world at all, they must be seen as *having their source in/ as being manifestations of* the Absolute, which may reflect badly on It.

So, there are at least a few reasons to question the idea that pro-pantheism is easily inferred merely by pantheism's conception of the Absolute as divine. Divinity, it is true, is usually taken as a value-laden term, in fact as a term implying infinite value. But as noted in the first point, there are reasons to think that, even if this holds true of the Absolute, it is not immediately evident that that would entail pro-pantheism rather than neutralism (on which the value of a pantheist world is viewed as equivalent to the value of a naturalist world). And in the second and third points, the potential for an agnosticism or even anti-pantheism becomes apparent.

However there are other grounds for advocating pro-pantheism, beyond the fact that it affirms the reality of divinity. Most notably, one might argue that the profound integration of all things entailed by this version of pantheism itself implies a very high degree of value, on the assumption that unity is a source of value. Order and structure, for example, can be seen as modes of unification, such that to the extent one values order one will value unity.

But there are complications here too. One might not share the normative intuition that unity/integration is ipso facto an indication of value (perhaps one is more greatly enamored with *diversity*); moreover one might point out that there are naturalist ontologies that model the universe as highly unified (e.g., Schaffer's (2009) priority monism), such that it is not automatically clear that the value of unity must be more greatly instantiated in a pantheist world than a naturalist one.

Another possible justification for pro-pantheism might lie in the claim that the Absolute is valuable because it functions as the source or ground of all reality as we know it (whether by giving rise to the latter as illusion, or simply by being that which the latter manifests or participates in). This can indeed be seen as an indication of value, *if what it has been sourced is itself seen as valuable*. That will in turn depend on how one assesses the balance of value versus disvalue in our finite world—a contentious matter, to say the least. Moreover it is not immediately clear why the presence of a source or ground of reality as we know it would by itself render a pantheist world better than a naturalist world; by hypothesis, the latter has no distinct ontological source, and needs none. Is that existential independence an automatic sign of disvalue? Why?

Obviously there is a great deal more to be said here; however, space constraints demand that we move on to the second alternative theism. As such I will conclude this section with a tentative (*very* tentative) assessment: one should probably be an agnostic with respect to the axiological status of this version of pantheism vis-à-vis metaphysical naturalism. That is, given current evidence and arguments, it makes more sense to suspend judgment concerning the status of pantheism than to adopt one of the other five views. (I think agnosticism is preferable to quietism here insofar as I do not yet see a reason to be so pessimistic as to think that the question is in principle unanswerable.)

4 Polytheism

As with pantheism, there are multiple understandings of/versions of polytheism. The one taken up here should again meet several desiderata: it should be non-naturalist, unambiguously distinct from other forms of theism and non-naturalism, and should have some precedent among actual world religions.

The first desideratum is easily met, since (unlike with pantheism) there are no self-styled "naturalist" versions of polytheism on offer. The second is trickier, insofar as historically polytheism has often been combined with pantheism or panentheism (whereby the One or the World-Soul has many literally existent finite-but-still-divine personifications/manifestations/emanations), and also with something akin to classical theism (whereby there is a single highest God but many subordinate divinities of lesser ontological status). However, there also seem to be many examples of what might be termed "pure polytheisms." These are polytheisms in which there are multiple divinities, all of whom are apparently of the same (typically finite) ontological status. One thinks for instance of the pantheons of ancient paganisms (Norse, Celtic, Greek, etc.) and some of their contemporary neo-pagan revivals; some Taoist and Shinto sects; and Mormonism.[21] Relatedly, the third desideratum is easily met, insofar as polytheism is ubiquitous across times and cultures.

Taking all that into account, I will assume that the type of polytheism under consideration may be formulated as follows: *multiple divinities exist, where divinities are understood as beings that are personal, either immaterial or possessed of a special kind of materiality (one not bound by the laws of physics), possessed of high though finite (and variable) degrees of power and knowledge, and which are variable in moral character.* Note that this formulation accords with Mavrodes's (2000) sixfold characterization of typical ancient polytheisms.[22]

One might suppose that a polytheist world would, all other things being equal, be better than a purely naturalist world on the ground that the instantiation of divinity must ipso facto add to the positive value of a world. However, complications arise here that are analogous to those encountered in the preceding discussion of pantheism, now compounded by the fact that none of the gods of polytheism is infinite in any way,[23] let alone infinite in perfection. As such it is not clear whether the mere presence of gods would supply enough value to outweigh automatically whatever intrinsic value is instantiated by a naturalist world, especially a sufficiently large, sufficiently populated, sufficiently well-ordered naturalist world.

Moreover, the common idea that "divinity" entails "deserving of worship" is false on polytheism, undermining still further the idea that the mere presence of divinities in a world would render that world better than a naturalist one. The gods are persons of variable character, and many polytheist religions feature gods that are wicked. Such gods are often worshipped nevertheless, not because they deserve it but on account of people's fearful need to placate their wrath, and/or a desire to curry their favor in order to facilitate a worshipper's own wicked acts (e.g., sacrificing to a god and then invoking its power to curse an enemy). Such beliefs and practices are not a feature of all polytheist religions, but they are common enough, and not ruled out by the formulation of polytheism we are working with. This feature of the view raises the prospect that if enough gods are evil enough, their presence may lessen the value of a world overall, and may lessen the well-being either of people generally or at least some persons (e.g., those on the receiving end of the curses). The moral variability of the gods thus raises the possibility that *wide anti-polytheism* (impersonal or personal) may be true, depending on the precise makeup of the divine pantheon. And the details really are important in this context; if most gods are virtuous but those gods are also less powerful than the few wicked gods, then people living in that polytheist world could still fare worse than they would have in a naturalist world. (Or rather, the good people living in that polytheist world could fare worse; for wicked people it might prove a boon, perhaps justifying a twin assessment of *wide anti-polytheism* plus *narrow personal pro-polytheism*.) On the other hand, if most gods are wicked but the few good gods are substantially more powerful than them, the resulting state of affairs might be such as to allow for a sunnier assessment, perhaps even *wide impersonal pro-polytheism*. The makeup of the pantheon is crucial.

The fact that in a polytheist world miracles are possible (the gods, even if embodied, can override the laws of physics) might be thought to lend any polytheist world sufficiently great value as to render pro-polytheism true regardless of the preceding concerns. But even if one takes the miraculous to entail some positive value, one needs to recall again that such a power in the hands of an evil god is liable to issue in bad consequences, perhaps sufficiently bad that their disvalue would outweigh the positive value of the mere existence and/or exercise of miraculous powers.

The conclusion we seem to be heading toward is the same (rather uninspiring) one reached in the discussion of pantheism: namely, *agnosticism*. Though here the agnosticism is motivated by the fact that rational advocacy of one or another of the axiological stances appears contingent on the acquisition of further information about the divine pantheon one is dealing with, information not supplied on the present model. What this may show is that polytheism is a philosophical view the evaluation of which (in axiological terms) cannot be prescinded from how that philosophical view is fleshed out in actual, concrete religious settings: that is, to make the assessment we really need to know whether we're assessing the Celtic pantheon versus the Taoist versus the Mormon and so on. Yet this is an interesting conclusion in its own right, and it serves to distinguish the axiological status of polytheism as quite different from that of (for instance) classical theism. For at least up to now, the various parties to the debate over the axiology of classical theism have mostly assumed that one can assess that philosophical view while abstracting from how it is instantiated in actual on-the-ground religious traditions (e.g., Judaism versus Islam).[24]

The only way I can see of trying to block an agnostic assessment of polytheism, and to affirm instead a generic pro-polytheism, would be to develop an *a priori* argument to the effect that any divinity (even a finite divinity of the sort envisioned on this formulation) must be morally good. Perhaps one could do so by denying that the gods have freewill (but then is it a mere lucky accident that their determinism is oriented toward value rather than disvalue?), or by denying that any being able to override the laws of physics could have any motivation to do evil. (Why rob a bank when you can simply manipulate lead into gold? For that matter who needs gold when you can work miracles?) However, the psychological plausibility of the latter suggestion is called into question by polytheistic religions themselves, with their many stories of miracle-working evil deities, not to mention the Christian story of the fall of powerful Lucifer. As such, I must again incline (tentatively) toward a conclusion of agnosticism.

Notes

1 By a "broadly classical" formulation of theism I simply mean the so-called omni-God formulation: God can be properly described as a personal, necessarily existent, inherently immaterial being who is omnipotent, omniscient, and omnibenevolent. (Note that the "properly described as" renders this statement of the formulation noncommittal with regard to whether these descriptions track really distinct divine attributes, or whether a robust formulation of the doctrine of divine simplicity obtains. It is also noncommittal as to whether the application of these descriptions should be understood as univocal, analogical, or as somehow apophatic.)

2 This will be evident from even a casual perusal of recent volumes of the major journals in the field. Sometimes it is also explicitly noted, including in the

axiological context; thus McLean (2015, 17) writes: "So I propose that, in considering theism, we think of the orthodox Christian story . . . and that, in considering atheism, we think of naturalistic atheism. . . . I suppose that many Western philosophers, and others, would regard those two views of the world as chief contenders in the metaphysical debate—as the two leading philosophical live options, as it were."

3 The recent anthology edited by Buckareff and Nagasawa (2016) is a nice example of this.
4 See Cooper (2006) for a detailed history of panentheism.
5 For a recent defense of a kind of animism, see Steinhart (2017). Note that he terms his view a form of naturalism, but this seems to me an implausible designation given the details of the ontology he lays out.
6 For an overview see Goff, Seager, and Allen-Hermanson (2017).
7 See Schellenberg (2005, 2007, 2009, 2013).
8 Of course, it may be that there are no two possible worlds in which theism is true of one and false of the other but where all else remains the same; indeed there may be no possible world in which much of anything remains the same, in the absence of God. Removing God from the picture might have dramatic and unavoidable "ripple effects," in particular given that the standard contrast in the current literature is with metaphysical naturalism, such that when removing God from the model typically no other nonnatural entities are introduced as replacements (like a pantheon of finite gods). Moreover if theism is necessarily true, then in fact there are no possible naturalist worlds anyway. These and related complications (e.g., the debate over whether metaphysical naturalism is compatible with any kind of objectivity/realism about value) are important and have received some attention within the existing literature; however, for ease of reference I here follow convention and leave such complications to one side, employing the simpler "all else being equal" formulation when providing an initial description of pro-theism and its rivals.
9 On this point see for instance Kahane (2011, 686).
10 Kahane (2011, 677–78) points to Albert Camus as an atheist who nevertheless advocates for pro-theism. He cites the following from Camus's *The Myth of Sisyphus*: "The certainty of a God giving meaning to life far surpasses in attractiveness the ability to behave badly with impunity. The choice would not be hard to make. But there is no choice, and that is where the bitterness comes in" (1942, 65). Of course, there may remain room for disagreement here; Rose (1994, 60–63) for instance maintains that, all things considered, Camus still warrants the label of "anti-theist," in company with such thinkers as Nietzsche, Proudhon, Bakunin, and Russell.

11 In putting forward this definition Steinhart cites for support the works of MacIntyre (1967, 34), Levine (1994), and Oppy (1997, n320).

12 Levine writes: "If pantheism is seen as the quintessential expression of divine immanence, then it is not difficult to see why it might be combined with panpsychism or animism. Like pantheism, both of these express a kind of pervasive immanence—'mind' in the former case and 'living soul,' 'spirit,' or 'animal life' in the latter. But however consonant or combined with pantheism these may be, they should be distinguished both from each other and from pantheism. . . . Animism, panpsychism, and especially the doctrine of a world-soul as embodied in the macrocosm/microcosm distinction, have at times been equated with pantheism. These positions may be intrinsic to particular versions of pantheism, but pantheism as such is broader than these and distinct from them" (2007, section 7). Relatedly, Sprigge's own preferred version of pantheism is explicitly also a form of panpsychism (1997, 202–5). And such taxonomic crosscutting is on display in several contributions to the Buckareff & Nagasawa (2016) anthology. For instance, Forrest (2016, 22)) labels the view he is discussing as a form of pantheism while also claiming Grace Jantzen's ontology as a predecessor, even though Jantzen's view has often been labeled a form of panentheism; Pfeifer (2016) develops a view that is obviously both pantheist and panpsychist (and which might also plausibly be classed as a form of panentheism); Leslie (2016) puts forward a view he labels pantheist but which (in my opinion) could just as easily be classed as panentheist and/or polytheist; and Nagasawa (2016) lays out a new version of panentheism which he notes could just as easily be classed as a type of pantheism.

13 Sprigge here footnotes Schrodinger (1964) and Picton (1904).

14 Consider, for instance, the vexed question of the precise existential status of the "illusions" or "presentations" of material objects and finite minds vis-à-vis the Absolute. Debates over this aspect of the theory might be viewed as analogous to debates surrounding the precise existential status of changeable material objects vis-à-vis the *real* beings (namely, the Forms) in Plato's system. (Thus Leftow's (2016) above-noted attribution of an outright eliminativism to Advaita Vedanta is debatable.)

15 Leftow, for instance, writes that "to be God, something must deserve worship" (2016, 70). He takes this an opening premise to argue that a purely naturalist pantheism is unworkable. Steinhart makes a similar point, employing it as part of an argument for the general superiority of non-naturalist over naturalist forms of pantheism (2004, 70).

16 See Davison (2012) for a compelling defense of that idea.

17 The editor rightly points out here that a pantheist could press this point further by noting that in a naturalist world containing an infinite number of beings, *each of those beings is itself finite*; as such, no *single* being would count as infinite, and so no single being would be a proper analogue to the Absolute. And perhaps it is unfair or misleading to compare the value-totals of a multitude of objects with that of a single object. However, in the face of that concern one might put forward for comparison a model of naturalism on which B-theoretic spacetime substantivalism is true and spacetime is infinite (i.e., a model where space extends infinitely in every direction, time has no beginning or end, and past/present/future are all equally real). That way there would be at least one natural object that could plausibly be called infinite, namely, the substance that is spacetime itself. Of course, it may be that such an entity could still not properly be compared to the Absolute; one might still press the claim that the value status of the latter is incommensurable with the value status of any natural object(s). But at least the problem of comparing a multitude with a unity would be sidestepped.

18 It is perhaps worth recalling here that a pantheist, unlike the classical theist, cannot fall back on any claims to the effect that the personhood of the Absolute grants it a unique kind of value, or on the claim that the perfect moral righteousness of the Absolute does so. The Absolute is nonpersonal.

19 One should hesitate to make the stronger claim that its status is inscrutable *for everyone necessarily* (thereby implying quietism rather than agnosticism). Hindu practice after all holds out hope that through meditation and/or devotional practices one can be united to the Absolute and thereby come to a nonconceptual, experiential realization of Its nature (and by extension Its value).

20 Note again a contrast with classical theism: while the classical theist is faced with the task of explaining how a good God could be justified in permitting evil, God's ontological distinction from the world at least guarantees a modicum of separation from/transcendence of that evil. The problem for the classical theist, in other words, is God's alleged aloofness from evil. The problem for the pantheist is God's apparent immersion in it/partial identity with it. Which problem is more worrying may be difficult to assess. Assessment is further complicated by the fact that most religions affirming classical theism also affirm an eschatological scheme whereby God finally puts a halt to evil and recompenses our suffering. On pantheism by contrast there is no guarantee that evil can or will come to an end.

21 For an accessible introduction to Western neo-paganism see Adler (1986). For a recent philosophical defense of neo-pagan polytheism see Greer (2005). For a

discussion of Taoist polytheism see Wong (1997), and on Shintoism Yamakage (2006). On Mormon polytheism see Bushman (2008) and Givens (2014). Note, however, that within these groups, too, diversity can be found; some within these traditions adhere to pure polytheism, and others to combinations of polytheism with alternative forms of theism or non-naturalism. (Adler (1986, ch. 3) is particularly helpful on the issue of philosophical diversity within neo-paganism.) The picture is further complicated by the fact that in some traditions (like Shintoism) the line between animism and polytheism (i.e., belief in nature spirits versus belief in gods) can become blurred. Mormonism in fact constitutes the "purest" of the pure polytheisms among major religious traditions today, being subject to no such combinations or blurring, at least if one is considering official LDS doctrine. (Individual Mormon believers by contrast sometimes tend to downplay their religion's commitment to polytheism; moreover, there are many schismatic groups that self-identify as Mormon but have broken away from the central LDS church, and whose theologies can differ in a variety of ways.)

22   Mavrodes's work remains one of the few detailed treatments of polytheism within the mainstream analytic literature. One might uncharitably assume that this lack of attention is warranted, with polytheism being ipso facto philosophically unsophisticated and devoid of any accompanying natural theology that might provide it a modicum of rational warrant. As it happens I disagree with that negative assessment and, space permitting, would discuss some arguments in its favor.

23   A qualification: the formulation of polytheism just provided was deliberately neutral on whether the gods were subject to generation and destruction, so it is left open whether any of them are infinitely old. Certainly, in some polytheistic religions the gods are manifestly mortal, being subject to birth and death.

24   Though see Dumsday (2016) for a challenge to that assumption.

Bibliography

Adler, Margot. (1986), *Drawing Down the Moon: Witches, Druids, Goddess-Worshippers, and Other Pagans in America Today*. New York: Penguin.

Alternative Concepts of God: Essays on the Metaphysics of the Divine. (2016), edited by Andrei Buckareff and Yujin Nagasawa. Oxford: Oxford University Press.

Bushman, Richard. (2008), *Mormonism: A Very Short Introduction*. Oxford: Oxford University Press).

Camus, Albert. (1942), *The Myth of Sisyphus*. London: Penguin.

Cooper, John W. (2006), *Panentheism: The Other God of the Philosophers—From Plato to the Present*. Grand Rapids: Baker Academic.
Davison, Scott. (2012), *On the Intrinsic Value of Everything*. London: Continuum.
Dumsday, Travis. (2016), "Anti-Theism and the Problem of Divine Hiddenness," *Sophia* 55: 179–95.
Forrest, Peter. (2016), "The Personal Pantheist Conception of God," in *Alternative Concepts of God: Essays on the Metaphysics of the Divine*, edited by Andrei Buckareff and Yujin Nagasawa, pp. 21–40. Oxford: Oxford University Press.
Givens, Terryl. (2014), *Wrestling the Angel: The Foundations of Mormon Thought—Cosmos, God, Humanity*. Oxford: Oxford University Press.
Goff, Philip, William Seager and Sean Allen-Hermanson. (2017), "Panpsychism," *The Stanford Encyclopedia of Philosophy* (Winter 2017 Edition), edited by Edward N. Zalta. URL = https://plato.stanford.edu/archives/win2017.
Greer, John Michael. (2005), *A World Full of Gods: An Inquiry into Polytheism*. Tucson: ADF Publishing.
Hedley, Douglas. (1996), "Pantheism, Trinitarian Theism and the Idea of Unity: Reflections on the Christian Concept of God," *Religious Studies* 32: 61–77.
Kahane, Guy. (2011), "Should We Want God to Exist?" *Philosophy and Phenomenological Research* 82: 674–96.
Kraay, Klaas. (2018), "Invitation to the Axiology of Theism," in *Does God Matter? Essays on the Axiological Consequences of Theism*, edited by Klaas Kraay, pp. 1–35. New York: Routledge.
Kraay, Klaas and Chris Dragos. (2013), "On Preferring God's Non-Existence," *Canadian Journal of Philosophy* 43: 157–78.
Leftow, Brian. (2016), "Naturalistic Pantheism," in *Alternative Concepts of God: Essays on the Metaphysics of the Divine*, edited by Andrei Buckareff and Yujin Nagasawa, pp. 64–87. Oxford: Oxford University Press.
Leslie, John. (2016), "A Way of Picturing God," in *Alternative Concepts of God: Essays on the Metaphysics of the Divine*, edited by Andrei Buckareff and Yujin Nagasawa, pp. 50–63. Oxford: Oxford University Press.
Levine, Michael. (1994), *Pantheism: A Non-Theistic Conception of Deity*. London: Routledge.
Levine, Michael. (2007), "Pantheism," *The Stanford Encyclopedia of Philosophy* (Summer 2007 Edition), edited by Edward N. Zalta. URL = http://plato.stanford.edu/entries/pantheism.
MacIntyre, Alasdair. (1967), "Pantheism," in *The Encyclopedia of Philosophy*, edited by P. Edwards. New York: Macmillan.
Mavrodes, George. (2000), "Polytheism," in *The Philosophical Challenge of Religious Diversity*, edited by Philip Quinn and Kevin Meeker, pp. 139–60. Oxford: Oxford University Press.

McLean, G .R. (2015), "Antipathy to God," *Sophia* 54: 13-24.

Nagasawa, Yujin. (2016), "Modal Panentheism," in *Alternative Concepts of God: Essays on the Metaphysics of the Divine*, edited by Andrei Buckareff and Yujin Nagasawa, pp. 91-105. Oxford: Oxford University Press.

Oppy, Graham. (1997), "Pantheism, Quantification, and Mereology," *Monist* 80: 320-36.

Pfeifer, Karl. (2016), "Pantheism as Panpsychism," in *Alternative Concepts of God: Essays on the Metaphysics of the Divine*, edited by Andrei Buckareff and Yujin Nagasawa, pp. 41-49. Oxford: Oxford University Press.

Picton, J. Allanson. (1904), *The Religion of the Universe*. London: Macmillan.

Rose, Seraphim. (1994), *Nihilism: The Root of the Revolution of the Modern Age*. Platina: St. Herman of Alaska Brotherhood.

Schaffer, Jonathan. (2009), "Spacetime the One Substance," *Philosophical Studies* 145: 131-48.

Schellenberg, J. L. (2005), *Prolegomena to a Philosophy of Religion*. Ithaca: Cornell University Press.

Schellenberg, J. L. (2007), *The Wisdom to Doubt: A Justification of Religious Scepticism*. Ithaca: Cornell University Press.

Schellenberg, J. L. (2009), *The Will to Imagine: A Justification of Skeptical Religion*. Ithaca: Cornell University Press.

Schellenberg, J. L. (2013), *Evolutionary Religion*. Oxford: Oxford University Press.

Schrodinger, Erwin. (1964), *My View of the World*. Cambridge: Cambridge University Press.

Sprigge, T. L. S. (1997), "Pantheism," *Monist* 80: 191-217.

Steinhart, Eric. (2004), "Pantheism and Current Ontology," *Religious Studies* 40: 63-80.

Steinhart, Eric. (2017), "Spirit," *Sophia* 56: 557-71.

Wong, Eva. (1997), *Taoism: An Essential Guide*. Boston: Shambhala Publications.

Yamakage, Motohisa. (2006), *The Essence of Shinto: Japan's Spiritual Heart*, translated by Mineko Gillespie, Gerald Gillespie, and Yoshitsugu Komuro. Tokyo: Kodansha International.

Commentary on "The Axiology of Theism: Expanding the Contrast Classes"

Michael Almeida

The project of axiological theism has largely focused on assessing the value of worlds in which the traditional God exists.[1] The traditional God is the Anselmian God—the God of perfect being theism. The God of perfect being theism provides an especially good object for evaluation since the provenance of the traditional God is deep in the history of Western philosophy and theology. The conception of God as a perfect being is central to monotheistic religions, of course, but the view has a much longer history. We find perfect being theology in Greek and Roman philosophers and other early thinkers including Zeno, Cicero, Chrysippus, Plato, Aristotle, Boethius, and St. Augustine. So the axiological question has implications for the Western theological and philosophical tradition.

The God of perfect being theism is an extraordinarily valuable being. Plato assumes that gods are the best possible beings.[2] Aristotle assumes that God must be the best substance.[3] The early Stoic Zeno argued that God is rational, wise, happy, and eternal, and everything it is better to exemplify. St. Anselm aimed to derive all of the attributes of God from a single premise that God is a being than which none greater can be conceived. God is, according to St. Anselm, *everything it is better to be than not be*. So, the research project of axiological theism is perfectly apt for the traditional God. The project challenges a fundamental tenet in Western theological and philosophical thought on the axiological import of God. God is, in Georg Cantor's terms, absolutely infinite in value and God confers infinite value on any world He inhabits.[4] The research project asks whence the value of the absolutely valuable being. The question is a serious challenge to a conception of God with deep historical roots.

Of course, not all metaphysical worldviews purport to confer value on worlds—or the inhabitants of worlds—in which they are true. Is it a criticism of such a view that it wouldn't be better overall were it true? It is difficult to see why it would be. Travis Dumsday considers two broad religious views—

pantheism and polytheism—that are at least ambiguous on the axiology of the divine. The sort of pantheism that Dumsday is interested in evaluating is a version of Advaita Vedanta.

The natural world and the multiplicity of conscious beings is an illusion, or at least a mere presentation, given to itself by a single Absolute which may be called "God" or at least plays something of the role of God for this point of view. Salvation consists in consciously realizing one's identity with this Absolute. The world of daily life, both physical nature and all its conscious inhabitants, is an illusion which one ultimate spiritual reality gives itself. Our salvation consists in our grasping the illusory nature of our world and of our separate existence and experiencing our identity with the One from which we were never really separate. This is the position of Advaita Vedanta as elaborated by Sankara. It is also the view of Erwin Schrodinger and in effect that of the almost forgotten, but highly interesting, Christian evolutionary pantheist Allanson Picton.[5] And though Vedanta offers an account of salvation—the soteriology of release from illusion—there is nothing in the account that suggests that God or the Absolute is an especially valuable being, or even purports to be an especially valuable being. Dumsday notes, for instance, the following:

> Thinkers within the Advaita Vedanta tradition have commonly claimed that the Absolute exceeds all our conceptual categories, such that none of our predicates—including our normative predicates—can be applied to it literally. As such one might claim that the value status of a pantheist world vis-à-vis a naturalist world is simply inscrutable for us at present, thereby providing a justification for agnosticism rather than pro-pantheism. (66)

But supposing we can sensibly ask value questions, the difficulty for the axiological issue is in deciphering the extraordinary metaphysics of the Vedanta doctrine. Suppose the soteriology described above is correct and we are all finally identical to the Absolute. We can surely come to the immediate conclusion that the properties of the Absolute are just the properties of the rest of us since, after all, the Absolute is literally identical to each of us. But what interesting value proposition could follow from that? Dumsday envisages something like a value explosion:

> If, for instance, I am awed by the vast grandeur of our galaxy, and (plausibly) interpret that response as indicative of some objective value possessed by our galaxy, then the fact that I am in some sense identical with the galaxy

may mean that my own value status is thereby heightened. The fact that the galaxy in turn is in some sense identical with God by extension may lend both it and me a still more exalted value status—presumably an *infinite* value status. (65)

The value of the Absolute would presumably supervene on (or, be grounded in) the properties the Absolute exemplifies, perhaps properties (roughly) analogous to the great-making properties of the traditional God. But there are no such analogous properties, so the ground of value for the Absolute is not at all obvious. But supposing again that the Absolute does have value, why would we conclude that the value of the Absolute is infinite? Notice that the reasoning in the passage just above won't do. The passage concludes on the basis of an identity claim—namely, that we are the Absolute—that since the Absolute is presumably infinite in value, then so are we. Following this line of reasoning, we might add that, since we are (more than presumably) finite in value, and since we are the Absolute, the Absolute is finite in value. Contradiction! The structure of the reasoning for each conclusion is the same and we have arrived at a contradiction. The reasoning is unsound.

So, what is the value of the Absolute? The extraordinary metaphysics of the Vedanta doctrine makes is difficult to tell. Reductive, non-eliminative identity claims are difficult to keep coherent in the easiest case of simple two-place identities. But it is fundamental to Vedanta that each of us is literally identical to the Absolute and so with one another. If that metaphysical picture is coherent, we are left to speculate on whether it would be good. It is fair to say that it would be difficult to know. Dumsday comes to something like that conclusion:

> I will conclude . . . with a tentative (*very* tentative) assessment: one should probably be an agnostic with respect to the axiological status of this version of pantheism vis-à-vis metaphysical naturalism. That is, given current evidence and arguments, it makes more sense to suspend judgment concerning the status of pantheism than to adopt one of the other five views. (69)

But as we noted at the outset, it is not a central aim of Advaita Vedanta to provide a metaphysical view that is maximally valuable or that includes an extremely valuable being. It does aim to provide the correct metaphysical picture of reality, however good that news would be. So, the fact that we can reach an at best agnostic conclusion on the axiological status of Advaita Vedanta might not constitute any problem at all for the view.

Dumsday also considers the axiology of a version of polytheism that satisfies the following description:

> The type of polytheism under consideration may be formulated as follows: *multiple divinities exist, where divinities are understood as beings that are personal, either immaterial or possessed of a special kind of materiality (one not bound by the laws of physics), possessed of high though finite (and variable) degrees of power and knowledge, and which are variable in moral character.* (70)

It is not a promise of the polytheistic metaphysical picture that polytheistic worlds would be especially valuable. The divine beings in polytheistic worlds are not essentially good beings and they do not exemplify the traditional theistic perfections. Indeed, the morally unrestrained deities in polytheistic worlds could be the source of much more evil than good. But it is again not a goal of polytheism that worlds including multiple deities of variable moral disposition would be better than a world without such deities. Arriving at the conclusion that we simply don't know how good a polytheistic world isn't especially bad news for a view that does not make bold axiological claims. So it is not unexpected that Dumsday arrives at such a conclusion:

> The conclusion we seem to be heading toward is the same . . . reached in the discussion of pantheism: namely, *agnosticism*. Though here the agnosticism is motivated by the fact that rational advocacy of one or another of the axiological stances appears contingent on the acquisition of further information about the divine pantheon one is dealing with, information not supplied on the present model. (71)

Dumsday's discussion of the axiology of pantheism and polytheism is illuminating and I think he arrives at the right conclusions. We should be agnostic on the value of these views—no matter which dimension of assessment we are considering. It also raises the issue of worldviews that aim to provide an account of metaphysical reality that is true, but not especially good news. It is difficult to know how theoretically damaging it would be to learn that such are axiologically unwelcome.

Notes

1 For discussion of some of the dimensions along which we might evaluate God's existence see Kraay 2018.

2 See Republic II, 381c.
3 See Metaphysics XII, 9, 1074b.
4 See Georg Cantor on the discovery of the absolutely infinite and its theological implications:

> What surpasses all that is finite and transfinite is no "Genus"; it is the single and completely individual unity in which everything is included, which includes the "Absolute" incomprehensible to the human understanding. This is the "Actus Durissimus" which by many is called "God." (Cantor 1908)

See also Dauben 1977 and Newstead 2009.

5 Sprigge 1997.

Bibliography

Aristotle. (2016), *Metaphysics*. UK: Hackett Publishing.
Cantor, Georg. (June 20, 1908), "Letter to G. C. Young," in Joseph Warren Dauben (1979), *Georg Cantor: His Mathematics and Philosophy of the Infinite*. Cambridge: Harvard University Press.
Dauben, Joseph W. (1977), "Georg Cantor and Pope Leo XIII: Mathematics, Theology, and the Infinite," *Journal of the History of Ideas* 38 (1): 85–108.
Does God Matter?: Essays on the Axiological Consequences of Theism. (2018), edited by Klaas Kraay. New York: Routledge.
Newstead, Anne. (2009), "Cantor on Infinity in Nature, Number, and the Divine Mind," *American Catholic Philosophical Quarterly* 83 (4): 533–53.
Plato. (2000), *The Republic*. Dover publications.
Sprigge, T. L. S. (1997), "Pantheism," *Monist* 80: 194.

Commentary on "The Axiology of Theism: Expanding the Contrast Classes"

Perry Hendricks

In his chapter, Dumsday considers the axiology of alternative forms of theism. He takes pantheism to be the view that multiple divinities exist, where the divinities have a high but finite amount of power, and where the divinities vary in respect to their moral character. And he takes pantheism to be the view that there exists only an Absolute nonpersonal being, meaning that there are not multiple distinct conscious creatures. The apparent existence of distinct conscious creatures is merely an illusion. In respect to whether pantheism would be better than naturalism, he holds to agnosticism. He says, "As such I will conclude this section with a tentative (very tentative) assessment: one should probably be an agnostic with respect to the axiological status of this version of pantheism vis-à-vis metaphysical naturalism" (69). He takes as a similar position in respect to the question of whether we should prefer polytheism to naturalism. That is, he thinks we should be agnostic about whether polytheistic worlds are better than naturalistic worlds.

I have no qualms with Dumsday's agnostic stance in respect to his position on the axiology of polytheism: agnosticism seems to be a plausible position about whether polytheism is preferable to naturalism. However, it does seem that there is (at least) one good reason to prefer a pantheistic world to a naturalistic one: in a pantheistic world, no rights are violated, and no one ever wrongs another person. This is because in a pantheistic world, there are no distinct persons, there is only the Absolute. Or, at the very most, if there are rights violated, it is only the Absolute violating its own rights. Either way, the world would be significantly better than a naturalistic world, in which the rights of distinct persons are *actually* violated. And this gives us reason to endorse impersonal pro-pantheism—the view that a pantheistic world is better than naturalistic worlds overall.

In addition to endorsing impersonal pro-pantheism, it seems that there is a strong case to be made for personal anti-pantheism—the view that the world is worse for (at least) some persons if it turns out to be pantheistic instead of naturalistic. The idea here is very simple: it is better to exist than to not exist.[1] If our world is naturalistic, then all apparently distinct persons are actual persons. However, if our world is pantheistic, then all apparently distinct persons are not persons at all: they do not exist—only the Absolute exists. For all the apparently distinct persons in our world whose lives are worth living, the world would be *worse* if it ended up being pantheistic since it would mean they do not actually exist. And hence personal anti-pantheism is true. Interestingly, this also provides us with reason to prefer a polytheistic world to a pantheistic world: in a polytheistic world, apparently distinct persons really exist, but in a pantheistic one they do not. And hence we should be personal pro-polytheists.[2]

What the above arguments show is that we should not be complete agnostics about the axiology of pantheism: we have some reason to endorse impersonal pro-pantheism and some reason to endorse personal anti-pantheism. But there is more we can say about the axiology of pantheism and polytheism if we compare them to classical theistic worlds—worlds in which an omnipotent, omniscient, and omnibenevolent God exists. This is an interesting topic that Dumsday does not explore. Here, I will briefly consider an argument that purports to show that classical theistic worlds are impersonally better than polytheistic and pantheistic worlds, that is, an argument for impersonal pro-classical theism.[3]

Alvin Plantinga (2004) has argued for impersonal pro-classical theism as follows.[4] God is perfectly good, meaning that there is no nonlogical limit to his goodness. As such, any world in which God exists will be infinitely good (since he exists in it), and therefore better than a world in which he does not exist. Now, neither the polytheism nor the pantheism that Dumsday considers entail anything that is infinitely good: polytheism posits finite gods, and pantheism makes no claims about the goodness or value of the Absolute. So, a classical theistic world will be impersonally better than a pantheistic or polytheistic world. And hence impersonal pro-classical theism is true.[5]

It seems that most arguments for variations of pro-theism can also be used as arguments for pro-classical theism over pantheism and polytheism. For example, Penner and Lougheed (2015) argue that adding morally good agents to a situation improves its overall value. Since God is a morally perfect agent, this means that the world would be better if he exists, and hence pro-classical theism is secured.[6] Since neither polytheism nor pantheism entail that there is a morally good agent, neither one can make use of Penner and Lougheed's argument. However, this argument meshes well with classical theism, since classical theism entails that there is a morally perfect agent. And hence we have another argument for pro-classical theism over pantheism and polytheism. Again, it seems that this can be done with almost any other pro-theistic argument.

Most of my reply has not been critical of Dumsday's chapter. The primary purpose of this reply has been to illustrate a path forward in respect to the axiological question about pantheism and polytheism. In addition to defending an argument for impersonal pro-pantheism and an argument for personal anti-pantheism, I have argued that we should consider the axiology of pantheism and polytheism in relation to classical theism.

Notes

1. This assumes the falsity of anti-natalism—the view that it would be better to not exist. Those who are anti-natalists can reconstruct the argument I give below as being for personal pro-pantheism.
2. More specifically, we should be personal pro-polytheists if the alternative is a pantheistic world. If the alternative is a classical theistic world (explained below), then we do not have reason to be personal pro-polytheists, since apparently distinct persons exist in a classical theistic world as well.
3. This is what is normally referred to as "pro-theism." I add the qualification "classical" to further distinguish it from pro-polytheism and pro-pantheism.
4. To be clear, his chapter is primarily concerned with defending the felix culpa theodicy, not with the axiology of theism.
5. This same argument also shows classical theistic worlds to be more valuable than naturalistic worlds (see Chapter 4 for more on this). And this allows us to construct the following ranking of impersonal value: classical theism > pantheism > polytheism and naturalism. In this chain, classical theism is the most valuable and polytheism and naturalism the least valuable. Pantheism is taken to be more valuable than naturalism and polytheism on account of the above argument I gave for impersonal pro-pantheism.
6. In Chapter 4, I try to show that their argument falls prey to skeptical theism. However, whether their argument succeeds is not relevant here.

Bibliography

Penner, Myron A. and Kirk Lougheed. (2015), "Pro-Theism and the Added Value of Morally Good Agents," *Philosophia* Christi 7 (1): 53–69.

Plantinga, Alvin. (2004), "Supralapsarianism, or 'O Felix Culpa,'" in *Christian Faith and the Problem of Evil*, edited by Peter van Inwagen, pp. 1–25. Grand Rapids: Eerdmanns.

Commentary on "The Axiology of Theism: Expanding the Contrast Classes"

Graham Oppy

If naturalism is necessary, then it is impossible that there is anything divine. If it makes no sense to have desires about impossibilia, then there are no interesting questions about the attitudes that we ought to take toward divine things.

But we can pretend. Suppose we do. What might we pretend? As Travis Dumsday notes, one thing we might pretend is that there is an omni-God: a necessarily existent, personal, immaterial, omnipotent, omniscient, perfectly good creator of all else. But, as he also notes, there are many alternative things that we might also pretend. He focuses on some varieties of pantheism and polytheism, but notes that he could also have attended to varieties of animism, panpsychism, and ultimism.

There are some questions that arise for the cases that Dumsday considers. In particular, the version of pantheism that he settles on for discussion is of dubious intelligibility. ("The natural world and the multiplicity of conscious beings, is an illusion, or, perhaps, a mere presentation that the Absolute gives to itself. Salvation consists in realizing one's identity with the Absolute" (80). If I am the Absolute, then so is everyone else, including Travis. Moreover, if I am the Absolute and Travis is the Absolute, then I am Travis. But I am not Travis. So I am not the Absolute. Thus, if there is nothing but the Absolute, then I do not exist. But I do exist. So it is not the case that there is nothing but the Absolute. Yet, if the Absolute exists, then there is nothing but the Absolute. So the Absolute does not exist.) But, whatever we might think about pantheism, panpsychism, animism, polytheism, ultimism, and the like, there are other dimensions of difference that might also reward attention.

One thought that we might consider is that there is *governance* of natural reality. Should we want that to be the case? If there is governance of natural reality, then, depending upon the evidence that we focus upon, we might suppose that that government is incompetent, or indifferent and aloof, or perverse and cruel, or jealous and arbitrary, or the like. If our final judgment is that, if there is governance, then that governance has some among these characteristics, then it seems to me that we should not want it to be the case that there is governance. Suppose, however, that our final judgment is rather that, if there is governance, then that governance is at worst benign, and perhaps better than benign. Should we want that to be the case? Even if the governance is benign or better than benign, it is not clear that we should embrace it if it is, for example, autocratic or oligarchic. Given that there is no prospect that the governance is democratic—since, evidently enough, we are not parties to the governance—perhaps, in the light of the evidence that we have, we should want it to be the case that natural reality is anarchic.

Another thought that we might consider is that there is governance of natural reality that is *represented* on earth. There are many religions that claim to be appointed representatives of the governance of natural reality. It is worth focusing on what we know about the self-proclaimed representatives of the governance of natural reality. Consider, to take just one example, the findings of the Australian Royal Commission into Institutional Responses to Child Sexual Abuse. If, for example, Gerald Risdale was an appointed representative of the governance of natural reality, then that governance is manifestly incompetent, or callously indifferent, or viciously malevolent. Whichever way we slice it, there are pretty clearly reasons why, given the evidence that we have, we should not want it to be the case that any of the self-proclaimed representatives of the governance of natural reality actually are representatives of the governance of natural reality.

A third thought that we might consider is that there is *more for us to come*: E. E. Cummings was wrong in thinking that death is a period, rather than, say, a parenthesis. Perhaps we need to fill this thought out a bit more before we try to assess it. Are we to think that the more to come is more of the same? Are we to think that the more to come will involve some kind of radical reassignment for us? Are we to think that the more to come will involve some kind of radical transformation for us? Are we to suppose that the more to come will involve reward and punishment? Are we to suppose that the more to come will involve reward and punishment that it is completely out of proportion to the deeds that we have performed? And so on and so forth. Perhaps there are other dimensions to the thought that we also need to consider. How long will what is to come last? Will there be subsequent radical reassignments or radical transformations? Will the rewards and punishments be arbitrarily assigned? Is there governance of the domain in which there is more to come? Here is one way that someone might think about some of this. There is no more evidence for future lives than there is for past lives. Given that I have no evidence—and, in particular, no memories—that I had past lives, I have no reason to want it to be the case that I had past lives. So, given that I have no evidence that I will have future lives, why think that I nonetheless have some reason to want it to the case that I will have future lives? If I am quite happy with a past from which I am absent, why should I not be similarly happy with a future from which I am absent?

A fourth thought that we might consider is that *things are not as they seem*. Very roughly speaking, what is distinctive of naturalism is that, in the causal domain, it is committed to just those kinds of things for which there is expert agreement on their existence. Were it not for the fact that we are not all experts on all subject matters, what would be distinctive of naturalism, in the causal domain, is that it is committed only to those kinds of things to which everyone is committed. Thus, there is a sense in which naturalism is the yardstick for how things seem to us: naturalism is committed to just those kinds of things that is seems to us, considered collectively, that there are. Consequently, in that same sense, non-naturalists are committed to the claim that things are not as they seem: there are nonnatural kinds of entities whose existence evades a significant proportion of the experts among us and yet are known to those non-naturalists. Should we want it to be the case that there are kinds of entities whose existence evades a significant proportion of the experts among us and yet are known to some of us? Some philosophers I know answer this question affirmatively: they want it to be the case that there is what they call "mystery." I do not share their point of view. I think that we should want it to be the case that there is no "mystery"; we should want it to be the case that, if certain kinds of things exist and are known to some of us, then experts are able to achieve independent, non-collusive agreement on the existence of those kinds of things. We should want things to be as they seem.

Of course, the topics that I have discussed—whether we should want there to be governance of natural reality, whether we should want there to be governance of natural reality that is represented on earth, whether we should want there to be more to come, and whether we should want it to be that things are not as they seem—are only some among the topics that I might have discussed. Once we follow Dumsday's lead in expanding the "contrast classes," there is a vast range of "axiological" questions that open up to us. I agree with him that, once we have raised the question whether we should want classical theism to be true, we can also consider whether we should want alternatives to classical theism such as pantheism, polytheism, animism, panpsychism, and ultimism to be true. But I think that, if we go this far, we should go further. Moreover—although I have not tried to make a case for this here—I think that there is a sense in which the kinds of questions that I have been considering are more fundamental than the kinds of questions that Dumsday considers (though that is not to say that I think that it is any more likely that we will be able to find agreed answers to them.) At any rate, particular filled-out versions of classical theism, pantheism, polytheism, animism, panpsychism, and ultimism are very complex hypotheses that have among their entailments, the kinds of claims that I have turned my attention to here.

Reply to Commentaries on "The Axiology of Theism: Expanding the Contrast Classes"

Travis Dumsday

I am very grateful to my fellow contributors for their careful and insightful engagement with my work, and to the volume's editor for bringing us all together for this discussion. I will say just a few brief things by way of response to the commentaries on my chapter.

Michael Almeida worries that a factor further complicating the assessment of the axiological status of Vedantin-style pantheism is the more basic question of its metaphysical coherence. He is concerned that such a version of pantheism will quickly become embroiled in contradictions, in part because of a broader philosophical worry lurking in the background: namely, that generally speaking it is difficult to maintain the coherence of *reductive but non-eliminative* identity claims, especially many-one identity claims. Thus to say that all the particles in the cosmos are really identical to the Divine Absolute (without saying that the Divine Absolute is thereby rendered nonexistent) is analogous to saying that a set of particles arranged chairwise is identical to a chair (without saying that the chair is thereby rendered nonexistent). Just as the plausibility and even coherence of the latter sort of claim is the subject of much controversy within analytic metaphysics (i.e., the composition-is-identity debate), the former is vulnerable to much the same set of concerns.

I agree with Almeida that this sort of pantheism faces coherence worries, though given this analogy with the composition debate in current metaphysics it is also worth recalling that certain sections of the latter literature (namely, those defending the coherence of many-one identity) may supply pantheism with novel (at least to it) avenues of defense. Of course that in turn depends on just how close the analogy really is, and I am sure there would be debate about this among pantheists.

Relatedly, it seems to me that the metaphysics literature dealing with composition has not given much attention to the potential axiological implications of the main competing views. For example, if we think that the chair is valuable, can the same be said of a set of particles arranged chairwise? In other words, in cases of reductive but non-eliminative identity, does metaphysical identity entail axiological identity? Why or why not? (This may be further complicated in cases of extrinsic value—if the chair is valuable because it's a family heirloom and I like it, does that make the set of particles valuable? I may not even know it's composed of particles.) The really pressing applications of course arise when it comes to living things like us; I take it that some assume that the value of human beings would be much diminished if it were to turn out that we were reducible to (even if not eliminable in favor of) clouds of particles arranged peoplewise. But even if that were the correct *ontology* of people, would that fact automatically diminish our *axiological* status? This question could perhaps use some further discussion.

Perry Hendricks suggests that there are good reasons to favor impersonal pro-pantheism over and against my preferred agnosticism. Specifically, he argues that impersonal pro-pantheism is true because a world without rights violations is better than a world with them, and a pantheistic world would be a world without rights violations. Why? Because rights violations entail that one person has in some way wronged or harmed another, distinct person, and on pantheism there are no really distinct persons.

Notice that this sort of argument could be broadened out. Consider an analogue: impersonal pro-pantheism is true because a world without many distinct pains is better than a world with them, and a pantheistic world would be a world without many distinct pains. Why? Because the reality of many distinct pains entails the reality of many distinct persons experiencing them (or at least one person existing over many distinct temporal moments), and on pantheism there are no really distinct persons or really distinct temporal moments.

I suspect pantheists themselves might see this kind of reasoning as too quick. As I noted, pantheists sometimes frame their view in such a way that finite beings (or "beings") are not wholly denied existential status, but instead are thought of as having a secondary existential status, as being mere illusions kicked up by a deeper reality or as being mere presentations/manifestations of a deeper reality. On such a framing, finite beings (whether distinct persons or distinct pains) are not absolutely unreal, they are not *nothing*. Rather, they are real in something like the limited, derivative sense in which the reflection in a mirror is real. Now, if it is ever legitimate to grant such limited, derivative realities (or "realities") any sort of axiological status, whether good or bad, then I think Hendricks's argument becomes problematic. As a matter of fact I think we are sometimes inclined to grant such things an axiological status (who among us has not disliked his reflection on occasion?), and for better or worse the Hindu intellectual tradition has certainly done so—the whole idea of a karmic system is based on sin and its punishment.

Something similar might be said with respect to Hendricks's comments on personal anti-theism: there is some sense in which the pantheist can affirm the existence—if limited and derivative—of the individual person, which could defuse his worry on that score.

In fairness to Hendricks though, it must be admitted that this way of framing pantheism (the finite-beings-as-reflections-of-God way) seems at least prima facie to be in tension with the alternative way of framing it, namely, in terms of *identity* (the finite-beings-as-identical-to-God way). My understanding of the Vedantin position is that these two modes of framing pantheism are viewed by its proponents as being compatible and complementary. However, to the critic it may end up making the view appear wily/slippery: when problems arise as a result of the identity-framing way of thinking about pantheism, the pantheist can simply shift to the reflection frame, or vice versa. Personally, I am unsure how to go about adjudicating this matter.

Graham Oppy has some similar worries about the coherence of this variety of pantheism, which worries again center around the identity-frame way of talking about the view. He then raises some larger axiological concerns that I take it are meant to apply to most versions of theism and/or supernaturalism, namely, concerns having to do with governance, the afterlife, and esotericism. I certainly agree that the questions raised are of considerable interest and importance. In particular, the questions Oppy raises regarding the non-public or esoteric status of certain alleged kinds of religious knowledge have been much neglected; although the distinction between exoteric and esoteric religions is well known and much discussed within the field of religious studies, it has received almost no attention within analytic philosophy of religion.

4

Skeptical Theism, Pro-theism, and Anti-theism

Perry Hendricks

1 Introduction

In the literature on the axiology of theism, there are primarily two positions taken: pro-theism and anti-theism.[1] Pro-theists hold that the world would, in some sense, be better if God exists; anti-theists hold that the world would, in some sense, be worse if God exists. Each of these positions can be subdivided: there are personal pro-theists, who hold that God's existence would make the world better for at least some persons; personal anti-theists, who hold that God's nonexistence would make the world better for at least some persons; impersonal pro-theists, who hold that God's existence would make the world better *simpliciter*; and impersonal anti-theists, who hold that God's existence would make the world worse *simpliciter*. And these positions can be further subdivided: "wide" or "narrow" can be applied to each of the above positions to indicate how strong "better" or "worse" is taken to be: the "wide" qualification specifies that the world is better (or worse) *overall*, or that some person's life is better (or worse) *overall*, if God does (or doesn't) exist; the "narrow" qualification specifies that the world is better (or worse) *in some respect*, or that some person's life is better (or worse) *in some respect*, if God does (or doesn't) exist. For example, a wide personal pro-theist holds that there are at least some persons whose lives would be better overall if God exists. Conversely, a narrow personal pro-theist holds that there are at least some persons whose lives would be better *in some respect* if God exists. Clearly, many of these positions are compatible: one can, for example, be both a personal pro-theist and a personal anti-theist.

I will not discuss any of the "narrow" positions. This is because the narrow positions can all be easily established. For example, suppose that Sally is an atheist: she believes that God doesn't exist. Further, suppose that theism turns out to be true. In such a world, God's existence has made Sally's life worse in a certain respect: she has a false belief (namely, her belief that atheism is true). This suffices to establish both narrow personal anti-theism and narrow impersonal anti-theism. But this isn't a very interesting result, and I know of no variant in which it becomes interesting.[2] And similar things can be said about all other pro-theist and anti-theist narrow positions. Therefore, I will not consider any of the "narrow" positions in the remainder of this chapter. All references to positions will refer to their "wide" versions.[3]

In this chapter, I'm going to consider personal and impersonal anti-theism and personal and impersonal pro-theism. I'll show that a position known as *skeptical theism* undermines arguments for personal anti-theism and impersonal anti-theism. On the other hand, I'll show that (at least some) arguments for personal and impersonal pro-theism are not susceptible to criticisms stemming from skeptical theism. This throws a wrench in many debates surrounding the axiology of theism: if skeptical theism is true, then it is very difficult to establish certain positions in answer to the axiological question about God.

2 Skeptical Theism and the Problem of Evil

Arguments from evil purport to show that some facts about evil that we know of either entail that God doesn't exist or at least make it improbable that he exists. Logical arguments from evil (e.g., Mackie 1955) attempt to do the former: they try to show that the existence of evil and the existence of God are incompatible, and since evil exists, it follows that God doesn't exist. Alternatively, evidential arguments from evil (e.g., Rowe 1979) try to show the latter: they argue that some facts about evil render God's existence improbable. Logical arguments from evil have been largely abandoned; many philosophers—both theists and atheists—think that God's existence is compatible with evil.[4] Therefore, much of the contemporary focus has been on evidential versions of the argument from evil, and in particular William Rowe's (1979) version. His argument (and others like it) makes use of something like the following inference:

1. We know of no good[5] that justifies God in allowing some instance of evil.[6]
2. Therefore, probably, there is no such good.

From (2), it is inferred that God probably doesn't exist, since God would not allow an instance of evil if there is no good that justifies him in doing so.[7] Many challenges have been given to premise (1): many philosophers offer *theodicies*; they argue that we know why God allows (at least some) evil (e.g., Plantinga 2004; Collins 2013, and Adams 1999). Alternatively, skeptical theists argue that the inference from (1) to (2) is dubious: that we don't know of a good that justifies God in allowing evil doesn't entail that there is probably no such good. And hence we cannot infer (2) from (1), and arguments from evil that rely on an inference like this are undercut: if the argument makes an inference from the goods (or evils) that we know of to the goods (or evils) that there are, its conclusion will be unmotivated.

There are various forms of skeptical theism,[8] but for the purposes of this chapter, I'll understand a skeptical theist to be a monotheist who affirms the following thesis:

> SKEPTICISM: We have no good reason for thinking that the goods and evils that we know are connected to some instance of evil are representative, in respect to their total value, of the actual goods and evils that are connected to said instance of evil.[9]

Goods and evils are taken to be states of affairs, and different states of affairs have different values. Take some disvaluable (bad) state of affairs X. If there's a sufficiently valuable (good) state of affairs Y that requires X, then Y (at least possibly) justifies one in allowing X. As such, SKEPTICISM amounts to the claim that we have no good reason for thinking that the states of affairs that we know are (causally) connected to some instance of evil are representative, in respect to their total value, of the actual states of affairs connected to the prior mentioned instance of evil. SKEPTICISM, it is held, undermines the inference from (1) to (2).[10] While atheists cannot be skeptical theists, skeptical theists think that *everyone*—theist or atheist—ought to endorse SKEPTICISM, and hence *everyone* ought to reject arguments from evil that rely on an inference similar to the one made from (1) to (2). But *why* should anyone accept SKEPTICISM? For accepting SKEPTICISM (or something like it), we are sometimes reminded of the fact that humans are cognitively limited creatures (Bergmann 2001; Alston 1991). Other times we're given analogies about parents and children, and reminded that (cognitively) we are like small children and God is like our parent (Wykstra 1984).

A more concrete reason to endorse SKEPTICISM is the following. Say that an *inscrutable* state of affairs is a state of affairs we know nothing significant about: all we know about an inscrutable state of affairs is that it's connected to some event, and other trivial facts (e.g., that it will happen in time, etc.). For any instance of evil we know of, we have no good reason to think that there aren't inscrutable states of affairs (causally) connected to it. (I will defend this below.) And if we have no good reason for thinking that there aren't inscrutable states of affairs connected to an event, then we have no good reason for thinking that the total value of states of affairs connected to the event that we know of are representative in respect to the total value of events actually connected to the event. This is because if the value of a state of affairs is inscrutable, then we have no good reason for thinking that it falls within the range of the values of the states of affairs that are connected to the event that we know of. And hence we have no good reason for thinking that all the states of affairs connected to the event fall within the same range. Indeed, if we did have such a reason, then we'd have good reason to think that there aren't any inscrutable states of affairs connected to the event. But we don't. And hence SKEPTICISM is secured.

The only contentious claim above is that we have no good reason for thinking that there are no inscrutable states of affairs connected to some event. Why should we think that's true? We should think that's true because many connections are separated by long periods of time, making it more difficult to perceive the connection. And, moreover, many connections have not yet occurred (such as the connections between current events and future states of affairs). Furthermore, some connections are complex and therefore difficult for humans to perceive. For example, many years ago, it wasn't obvious to anyone that smoking was connected to getting cancer: the connection between smoking and getting cancer was complex, and took some time to discern. Because of the complexity of connections and the fact that we cannot perceive future connections, we have no good reason to think that there aren't any inscrutable states of affairs connected to some event.[11] (Indeed, since we know that for any event we observe, there will very likely be distant states of affairs connected to it, we have good reason to think that there are inscrutable states of affairs connected to it). Conjoin this with the reasoning in the above paragraph, and we (both theist and atheist) have good reason to endorse SKEPTICISM. There's no doubt more to say here, but I don't have the space to say it.[12] Instead, I will be assuming the truth of SKEPTICISM for the remainder of this chapter. Anyone not convinced by the above argument can read this as a conditional: if skeptical theism is true, then certain arguments for personal and impersonal anti-theism are undermined.

3 Skeptical Theism and Anti-theism

3.1 Skeptical Theism and Personal Anti-theism

Personal anti-theism is the view that there are at least some persons of whom it would be better overall if God didn't exist. One argument for this view is called "the meaningful life argument." The meaningful life argument purports to show that if God exists, then at least some persons will lack a meaningful life, and if one's life lacks meaning if God exists, it's better for her that God doesn't exist.[13] Kirk Lougheed has developed an objective version of the meaningful life argument: he says that there is a set of objective goods "Os" which is "such that for every agent S pursuing or obtaining the goods in Os is necessary for S to have a meaningful life" (2017, 344). From here, he states the argument as follows:

3. If God's existence would constrain or prevent S from obtaining some of the goods in Os, then God's existence would constrain or prevent S from obtaining a meaningful life.
4. If God's existence would constrain or prevent S from obtaining a meaningful life, then it's rational for S to prefer that God doesn't exist.[14]
5. So, if God's existence would constrain or prevent S from obtaining some of the goods in Os, then it's rational for S to prefer that God doesn't exist.
6. God's existence would constrain or prevent S from obtaining some of the goods in Os.
7. Thus, it's rational for S to prefer that God doesn't exist. (Lougheed 2017, 344).[15]

But this argument needs to be revised. Here's why. First, let's grant that God's existence constrains or prevents S from obtaining a meaningful life. Next, suppose that there is some great good *for* S that would only obtain if God exists *and* that this good is so great that it would make S's life better for her than if she had a meaningful life. If this is the case, then S's life would be *worse* for her if she had a meaningful life. So, the question then is whether God's existence precluding (at least some of) the goods residing in Os brings about a greater good for S. This means that premises (4), (5), and (6) need to be amended as follows:

4*. If God's existence would constrain or prevent S from obtaining a meaningful life, then it's rational for S to prefer that God doesn't exist *provided that a greater good doesn't come about from S lacking a meaningful life.*
5*. So, if God's existence would constrain or prevent S from obtaining some of the goods in Os, then it's rational for S to prefer that God doesn't exist *provided that a greater good doesn't come about from S lacking a meaningful life.*
6*. God's existence would constrain or prevent S from obtaining some of the goods in Os *and a greater good doesn't come about from S lacking a meaningful life.*

The key premise of the objective meaningful life argument is now (6*). While Lougheed has defended his original version of the argument, he (unsurprisingly) hasn't defended this revised version. Thus, we cannot look to his work for a defense of (6*). So, how might one go about defending (6*)? One way would be as follows:

8. We know of no (greater) good that comes about from S lacking a meaningful life.
9. Therefore, probably, there is no such good.

From (8) and (9), we have reason to think that premise (6*) is probably true. It should be clear, however, that in the same way that the inference from (1) to (2) (see above) falls prey to SKEPTICISM, the inference from (8) to (9) also falls prey to SKEPTICISM: both are inductive inferences from the goods we know about to the goods that there are, and SKEPTICISM (we have assumed) undermines this type of inference. Therefore, this route will be of little use: skeptical theism precludes this route for advocates of the (revised) objective meaningful life argument. And hence skeptical theism leaves premise (6*), and therefore the conclusion of the argument, unmotivated.

An alternative route would be to mimic the so-called common sense problem of evil. The commonsense problem of evil (Dougherty 2008 and 2014) makes use of phenomenal conservative justification. The advocate of phenomenal conservatism holds that if it seems to S that p, then, in the absence of defeaters, S has (at least some) justification for believing p (Huemer 2007).[16] The idea behind the commonsense problem of evil is that there are some evils that *seem* gratuitous,[17] and this seeming provides justification for believing that it is, in fact, gratuitous.

In a similar manner, one might try to exploit phenomenal conservatism to justify personal anti-theism: she might claim that it *seems* to her that there is no greater good that comes about from her lacking a meaningful life, and that this justifies her in accepting personal anti-theism. While it's possible to quibble over whether S has a defeater for her seeming here, I'll grant that she doesn't, and see where it takes us. The fact is that it doesn't take us very far at all: that premise (6*) is justified for S doesn't mean it's justified for anyone else. And the revised objective meaningful life argument—like its predecessor—is meant to convince others that personal anti-theism is true: it's not merely supposed to show that it's *possible* that someone is justified in accepting its conclusion. In other words, the proponent of the objective meaningful life argument is concerned with showing that personal anti-theism is true, not merely showing that there can be phenomenal conservative justification for it.[18] And hence this route does not offer us much promise either.[19]

A final route to establish premise (6*) would be to show that a meaningful life is *unsurpassably* good for S. If a meaningful life is unsurpassably good for S, then, if God's existence precludes a good that's necessary for S to have a meaningful life, whatever good his existence brings about for S, it will not outweigh S's lacking a meaningful life. And hence personal anti-theism is true. A problem for this route is that a meaningful life doesn't seem to be a candidate for being an unsurpassable good for S: there are clear cases in which the world is better for S if she lacks a meaningful life instead of having a meaningful life. And this means that we cannot rule out the possibility of a greater good for S coming about from her lacking a meaningful life. A clear case of this can be seen by (slightly) embellishing the story of Herman Goering. Goering was a Nazi leader, who was very successful at his job prior to losing the Second World War. However, Eleonore Stump points out:

> None of us . . . would willingly trade lives with a moral monster such as . . . Goering, even if Goering had in fact been jovial or content, even if Goering had died before the Nazis lost the war. Just because Goering was a moral monster, we would not want to have had a life such as his. *So, even if Goering felt no remorse over the moral evil he did, his life suffered because of it.* (2010, 4, emphasis mine)

Stump's point is that because of who Goering became—because of the character he developed—his life was *worse for him* because he was successful. To see how this undermines the objective meaningful life argument, suppose that the meaning in Goering's life consisted of him doing his job well. A world in which Goering doesn't (or can't) do his job well is better *for him* than a world in which he does: it would be better overall for him to not be able to act in morally monstrous ways than to have a meaningful life consisting in performing immoral actions well. And hence it would have been better for Goering's life to lack meaning than for it to have meaning. This is why we wouldn't (or shouldn't) trade lives with Goering.

Perhaps, however, one holds that a meaningful life cannot be like Goering's: a meaningful life cannot involve performing heinous acts, such as those that were a part of Goering's life. Those who hold this view may consider a different example: suppose that S's life is meaningful, and that if God exists, her life will lack meaning. Suppose, however, that if God exists, S will spend eternity with him in heaven. In such a case, S's life would lack meaning if God exists, but she'd also gain an eternal and pleasant afterlife. In such a case, S's life would be better if God exists; she should prefer that God exists even though it would mean that her life lacks meaning. And this shows that a meaningful life is not an unsurpassable good: an eternal and good afterlife is more valuable than a meaningful life. Thus, the proponent of the revised meaningful life argument cannot use this route to motivate premise (6*).

In this section, we've seen that the most obvious ways to go about motivating premise (6*) are dubious. Whether there's another way to motivate (6*), I do not know. However, as things stand, we have no good reason to endorse (6*), and hence the meaningful life argument fails. This same problem will plague other attempts to establish personal anti-theism: such arguments must show that God's existence will prevent some valuable anti-theistic good from obtaining in S's life, and that there is no other good that comes about from God's existence that makes up for the prevention of the anti-theistic good.[20] However, as we saw above, skeptical theism makes this a difficult thing to show.

3.2 Skeptical Theism and Impersonal Anti-theism

Above, we saw that it's very difficult to establish personal anti-theism. The problem is that it's extremely difficult to show that there is no greater good that comes about from humans lacking certain anti-theistic goods, such as a meaningful life. This issue, however, also spells problems for *impersonal* anti-theism; the same problems that arise for personal anti-theism arise for impersonal anti-theism. This is because in order to motivate impersonal anti-theism, one would need to show that there are anti-theistic goods that are so valuable that the world is worse if God exists. But this will force the anti-theist to rely on something like the following line of reasoning:

10. If God exists, then we lack good X.
11. We know of no (greater) good that comes about from our world lacking X (or comes about from God's existence).

Therefore,

12. Probably, there is no such good.

However, it's clear that the inference from (11) to (12) is vulnerable to SKEPTICISM; skeptical theism undermines the inference from (11) to (12). And hence the impersonal anti-theist must find a different route to motivate (12).

The most obvious alternatives for the impersonal anti-theist to motivate (12) are to mimic the commonsense problem of evil (detailed in Section 3.1) or by identifying an unsurpassable anti-theistic good. If the impersonal anti-theist mimics the commonsense problem of evil, she is vulnerable to the same criticism raised against the personal anti-theist: she's trying to show that impersonal anti-theism is true, not merely that some persons possibly have phenomenal conservative justification for believing it. And hence this route will be of little use to her.

Perhaps, however, the impersonal anti-theist would have more luck identifying some unsurpassable anti-theistic good.[21] What might this good be? The usual anti-theistic goods discussed are the good of privacy and the good of autonomy.[22] However, neither privacy nor autonomy is a candidate for being an unsurpassable good. Consider first privacy:

> BULLY: Sarah is an anxious teenager. She has been becoming more and more distant at home, and her parents have taken notice. They are worried about her and try to talk to her about her sudden change in behavior. But Sarah won't open up. Her parents eventually become so worried that they go into her room when she's away and read her diary. They find out that she's been being bullied at school, and that this is causing her abnormal behavior. Her parents then go to the school principal and let him know about the bullying. The principal puts a stop to the bullying, and Sarah's life is now much improved.

BULLY is a pretty clear case in which a violation of privacy brings about a greater good: Sarah no longer being bullied while losing her privacy is better than her being bullied while continuing to have privacy. And this means that privacy is not a candidate for an unsurpassable good. In fact, it's easily surpassed.

So much for privacy. What about autonomy? Consider the following example:

> WOODS: Sally, a teenager, is hiking with her parents in the mountains. A storm unexpectedly hits them, and she becomes separated and lost. Her parents are unable to find her. For weeks, they bring in search teams to look for her, but she is not found. However, Sally is not dead: she's simply unlucky that she never crossed paths with the search teams. She lives on the mountain for a year on her own. During this year, she is completely autonomous: she chooses what she wants to do and when she wants to do it; there are no rules or authorities telling her what to do. Months later, she slips and hits her head on a rock, knocking her unconscious. Fortunately for her, a hiker stumbles upon her body, and brings her to a hospital. Once she's released from the hospital, she's reunited with her parents. However, once she returns home with her parents, she can no longer do whatever she wants whenever she wants: she must listen to her parents and follow their rules. However, Sally's life, though lacking autonomy, is now much improved.

WOODS straightforwardly shows that autonomy is not a candidate for an unsurpassable good: it is easily surpassed by other goods, such as being reunited with family. If there's any serious candidate for an unsurpassable anti-theistic good, I don't know of it. I leave it to the impersonal anti-theist to produce one. I conclude, therefore, that the prospects of motivating (12) by identifying an unsurpassable anti-theistic good are dubious.

In this section, I've argued that skeptical theism presents an obstacle to impersonal anti-theism: it makes it difficult to show that the world is better overall if God doesn't exist.

4 Pro-theism

4.1 How to be a Skeptical Theist *and* a Personal Pro-theist

Earlier, I argued that the objective meaningful life argument for personal anti-theism is undermined by skeptical theism. I further noted (fn 13) that one can make a similar objective meaningful life argument for personal pro-theism:

one might think that S's life would lack meaning if God doesn't exist, and that it's therefore better for S if God exists. However, this argument, too, falls prey to skeptical theism: a meaningful life is not an unsurpassable good (see Section 3.1), and it is difficult to show that there is no anti-theistic good that outweighs having a meaningful life: an appeal to phenomenal conservatism won't do the trick (for reasons given above), and neither will an inference from our lack of knowledge of an anti-theistic good that is more valuable than a meaningful life to the conclusion that there is no such good; skeptical theism precludes such inferences. And hence this route for establishing personal pro-theism isn't viable.

However, there's an alternative way to establish personal pro-theism that *isn't* vulnerable to skeptical theism. The way to do so is to identify a good for some persons that is unsurpassable for them. While I argued above that none of the purported anti-theistic goods are candidates for being unsurpassable goods for some persons (or for the world), the same isn't true for at least one pro-theistic good, namely, the good of being in union with God; if God exists, some persons will have union with him. To be in union with God is to have one's will aligned with God's will and to have communion with him. Understood this way, union with God is an unsurpassable good: to be in union with God is to be in union with one's creator, who is all powerful, all knowing, and all good. Nothing can be better for a person than to have this union. This view goes (at least) back to St. Thomas Aquinas, and is defended by Stump (2010). Describing and defending Aquinas's views, she says, "The unending shared union of loving personal relationship with God is the best thing for human beings; the worst thing is its unending absence" (2010, 388). This view is plausible and *at the very least* isn't obviously false: union with God is a genuine candidate for the greatest good for human beings, and unlike the good of privacy and the good of autonomy, there aren't obvious counterexamples to it. This shouldn't be understood as my inferring from there being no goods that we know of that are greater for a person than union with God to the conclusion that there is no such good. Rather, I'm saying that this appears to be an unsurpassable good for persons, and there aren't any goods for persons that can be plausibly thought to be more valuable than it. Thus, the personal pro-theist can plausibly claim that there are some persons that the world would be better for if God exists, since this would entail that they obtain an unsurpassable good (i.e., union with God). So, if there are any problems with this argument for personal pro-theism, it isn't that skeptical theism undermines it: we don't need to rely on an inductive inference to make this case for personal pro-theism, which was what caused trouble for the above-examined anti-theistic arguments.[23] And hence we have a route to establishing personal pro-theism that skeptical theists can make.

4.2 Skeptical Theism and Impersonal Pro-theism

Recall that impersonal pro-theism is the view that God's existence would make the world better overall. Myron Penner and Kirk Lougheed (2015) have argued for impersonal pro-theism on the grounds that God is a morally good agent, and that adding a morally good agent to a state of affairs increases its value.[24] They argue as follows:

13. For any state of affairs x, introducing a good moral agent S to x adds value to that state of affairs unless S is constrained in ways that prevent S from exercising effective morally good agency.
14. God is a good moral agent.
15. God is not constrained in ways that prevent God from exercising effective morally good agency.
16. So, for any state of affairs x, introducing God to x adds value to that state of affairs. (Penner and Lougheed 2015, 58)

Premise (13) is supported with an example: if my car is broken down, it's a good thing for a morally good agent to stumble across me since she would try to help me—though, of course, it's possible that her trying to help me makes my situation worse (e.g., while trying to change my tire, the morally good agent ends up puncturing my spare, leaving me worse off than I was before). While their support for (13) isn't terribly strong, the premise itself seems quite plausible, so I'll grant it. Premise (14) is true by definition. And this leaves us with only one premise remaining, namely premise (15). The rest of this section will consider this premise.

Why should we think that premise (15) is true? How is it that we *know* that God is not constrained from exercising effective morally good agency?[25] It can't be on the grounds that God's agency can't be constrained, for he may very well constrain his agency in order to obtain a good (or for some other reason). Indeed, Penner and Lougheed concede this point: they hold that God might, for example, constrain his agency in order to allow for libertarian freewill. They say: God "might not be able to exercise agency that would contribute to a better state of affairs when such agency would violate human [libertarian] freedom" (2015, 59, fn 12). So, if there's some good that requires God to constrain his agency, then God will (at least possibly) constrain his agency. But then how do Penner and Lougheed show that there isn't a good that restricts God's agency? They deal with this problem by saying that from the fact that there may be some constraints on God's ability to act, it doesn't follow that he's completely constrained, nor does it follow that "God exercising agency doesn't contribute far more value to the world than finite humans (even on the assumption [that] such agency is limited in certain ways)" (2015, 59, fn 12). This is fair enough: the fact that God might be constrained in some ways doesn't entail that he's completely constrained, and it doesn't follow that the ways in which God does act don't make the world better off overall. *However*, it equally doesn't follow that God *isn't* constrained in significant ways or that the ways that God does act make the world better off overall: there might be some good, akin to libertarian freedom, that requires God to nearly completely limit his agency, in which case he can add very little of value to the world *through exercising agency.* For example, suppose (contrary to what I have argued above) that privacy is an unsurpassable good, and that God largely restricts his knowledge in order to allow for privacy. Such a restriction (we may suppose) would greatly constrain his ability to effectively exercise agency. Indeed, it may constrain him so much that he's not able to add sufficient value to the situation to overcome the loss of privacy and other anti-theistic goods (e.g., autonomy).[26] In such a case, God would be constrained in such a way that he couldn't (significantly) exercise morally good agency, in which case premise (15) would be false. What this means is that, contra Penner and Lougheed, we can't just assume that some goods don't severely restrict God's agency. And this means that we can't just assume the truth of premise (15).

Given this, how could Penner and Lougheed motivate premise (15)? They would (at least) need to show that there aren't goods that require God to significantly constrain his agency. And how would they show that there aren't such goods? Presumably, they would need to infer from our lack of knowledge of a good that would require God to constrain himself to the conclusion that there is no such good. But, of course, this inference would fall prey to skeptical theism, and hence will not work. It's unclear how else one could motivate this premise, and this casts doubt on their argument: there's no clear way to motivate premise (15), and therefore we have no clear reason for accepting their argument.

4.3 How to be a Skeptical Theist *and* an Impersonal Pro-theist

While the Penner and Lougheed's argument for impersonal pro-theism was shown to ultimately fall prey to skeptical theism, there are other ways that skeptical theists can argue for impersonal pro-theism. In this section, I'll illustrate one acceptable way for skeptical theists to argue for impersonal pro-theism: I'll show that Alvin Plantinga's argument for impersonal pro-theism is immune to, and compatible with, skeptical theism. The purpose of this section isn't to defend Plantinga's argument; rather, it's merely to show that his argument doesn't succumb to skeptical theism and isn't itself obviously unsound.

Take God to be the greatest possible being: God possesses all great-making properties to the maximal degree.[27] One such property is *goodness*: God is *maximally* good; there is no nonlogical limit to God's goodness. This, according to Plantinga, means that any world that doesn't contain God will always be inferior in respect to value to a world that does contain God: no matter how great the creatures in a godless world act, no matter what virtues they cultivate, relationships they create, no matter what other events occur in such a world, it will always be less valuable than a world in which God exists. This simply follows from God being maximally good; if something other than God could be more valuable than him, then there would be a nonlogical limit to his goodness. In Plantinga's words: "God himself, who is unlimited in goodness, love, knowledge, power and the like, exists in [a theistic] world; it follows, I suggest, that the value of any state of affairs in which God alone exists is itself unlimited" 2004, 9. In other words, the value of a world in which God exists is unlimited, but the value of a world in which God doesn't exist is limited. And hence worlds in which God exists will always be more valuable than worlds in which he doesn't.[28] Does skeptical theism undermine this argument?

The answer, I think, is a clear "No": whatever problems one might have with Plantinga's argument, it isn't relevant to skeptical theism: Plantinga is not guilty of relying on an inference from the goods (or evils) we know of to the goods (or evils) there are. Instead, he *identifies* the greatest possible (and unlimited) good, and derives his conclusion from that. Perhaps one could dispute whether

God's goodness is unlimited, but that dispute will not be grounded in her skeptical theism. And hence Plantinga's argument for impersonal pro-theism is left untouched by skeptical theism. Thus, one can both endorse skeptical theism and defend impersonal pro-theism.

4.4 An Asymmetry: Why Is Skeptical Theism Compatible with Pro-theism but not Anti-theism?

While skeptical theism makes it extremely difficult to construct a case for both personal and impersonal anti-theism, it doesn't pose trouble for personal and impersonal pro-theism. What explains this asymmetry? Why is it that skeptical theism makes it difficult to make a case for personal and impersonal anti-theism but not for personal and impersonal pro-theism? The answer is that for both personal and impersonal pro-theism, there's a serious, plausible candidate for an unsurpassable pro-theistic good: namely, union with God (for personal pro-theism) and God himself (for impersonal pro-theism). This means that no inductive inference is needed on the part of the personal and impersonal pro-theist in order to argue for her position.[29] On the other hand, anti-theistic goods are clearly surpassable: privacy, autonomy, and so on are not plausible candidates for goods that cannot be improved upon. If the personal or impersonal anti-theist knew of a good that wasn't obviously surpassable, she might be able to construct an argument that—like (certain) pro-theistic arguments—is immune to skeptical theism. However, as things currently stand, the prospects of this are dubious: a candidate for an unsurpassable anti-theistic good is not forthcoming. And hence we are left with an asymmetry: one can easily endorse skeptical theism and personal and impersonal pro-theism, but it's difficult to see how one can endorse skeptical theism and personal or impersonal anti-theism.

5 Conclusion

In this chapter, I first examined arguments for personal and impersonal anti-theism. These arguments were shown to be vulnerable to skeptical theism; they depend on an inductive inference from the goods that we know of to the goods that there are, and as such were undercut by skeptical theism. After this,

I examined an argument for impersonal pro-theism, and showed that it, too, is vulnerable to skeptical theism. However, I showed that there are ways in which one can argue for both personal and impersonal pro-theism that don't rely on an inductive inference from the goods we know of to the goods we are, and hence are not vulnerable to skeptical theism. The way to do so is to, in respect to personal pro-theism, identify a pro-theistic unsurpassable good for persons; and in respect to impersonal pro-theism, one needs to identify a pro-theistic unsurpassable good *simpliciter*. Since there are plausible candidates for both types of pro-theistic unsurpassable goods, the case for pro-theism, both personal and impersonal, is not threatened by skeptical theism. This, however, results in an asymmetry between pro-theism and anti-theism: skeptical theism is compatible with the former but not (at least obviously) compatible with the latter.[30]

Notes

1 Pro-theism and anti-theism (and their variants) are not exhaustive: there is also, for example, indifferentism, which holds that God's existence wouldn't make a difference.
2 Kraay and Dragos (2013, 160) take narrow personal anti-theism to be the view that it would be *far worse* in some respect for at least some persons if God exists. The "far worse" qualification doesn't avoid my charge of uninterestingness: in my example, Sally's life is *far worse* in respect to her beliefs about the foundation of reality.
3 Because of this, I will omit the "wide" qualification for the remainder of this chapter: all positions spoken of should be assumed to be "wide."
4 For example, Peter van Inwagen says that "it used to be widely held that evil . . . was incompatible with the existence of God: that no possible world contained both God and evil. So far as I am able to tell, this thesis is no longer defended" (1991, 135) and Trent Dougherty says that "in the late 1970s, a consensus began to emerge that Alvin Plantinga . . . had buried the so-called 'logical problem of evil'" (2011, 560).
5 Goods and evils should be understood to be states of affairs.
6 Say that a good justifies God in allowing an instance of evil if and only if the evil occurring resulted (or will result) in a good that outweighs it, or that eliminating the evil would have brought about an evil equally bad or worse.
7 This assumption is no longer safe to make: it has been challenged by, for example, Hasker 2008; van Inwagen 2006; Sullivan 2013, and Rubio 2018.

8   See e.g. Cullison 2014; Hudson 2014, and Wykstra 1984.
9   SKEPTICISM is meant to track the skeptical theism of Michael Bergmann 2001, 2009, and 2012. I defend this understanding of Bergmann's skeptical theism in Hendricks (2019).
10 I don't have the space to discuss this normative assumption. See Bergmann 2001, Hendricks (2018b) and Hudson 2014, 2017 for a discussion of it.
11 See Durston (2000) for a similar point.
12 See Hendricks (forthcoming) for a more developed version of this argument.
13 It originated from Guy Kahane 2011, was elaborated and critiqued by Myron Penner 2015, further elaborated and defended by Kirk Lougheed 2017, and, finally, critiqued by Penner 2018.
14 It is assumed in this argument that if a world W is better for S than a world W*, that it's irrational for S to prefer W*.
15 Interestingly, one could revise the objective meaningful life argument and use it to support personal pro-theism: one might argue that the meaning of at least some persons' lives depends on God's existence. And hence if God doesn't exist, their life would lack meaning and, therefore, it would be better for them if God exists. I only examine the personal anti-theist version of the argument in this section. However, the personal pro-theist version of the argument would fail for the same reasons the personal anti-theist version does.
16 See also Chris Tucker 2011, 2013.
17 Where an evil is gratuitous just in case there is no good that justifies God in allowing in, see fn 6.
18 This is why we are offered the meaningful life *argument* for personal anti-theism: it is meant to show that there really are (at least possible) persons that would have better lives if God exists. If all the personal anti-theists were trying to show was that some persons have phenomenal conservative justification for the proposition *personal anti-theism is true*, then no argument would be needed.
19 This parallels the criticism I raise of the common sense problem of evil in Hendricks 2018a.
20 By "anti-theistic goods" I mean goods that only come about if God doesn't exist.
21 This is the route that Lougheed forthcoming considers and ultimately deems unsatisfactory (for different reasons).
22 See e.g. Kahane 2011; Lougheed 2017, 2018; Hendricks and Lougheed 2019, and Davis 2014.
23 If one could show that it's surpassable or not a plausible candidate for an unsurpassable good for persons, then skeptical theism might undermine it. But, again, this hasn't been done.

24 They think that their argument establishes all types of pro-theism. While I focus on impersonal pro-theism, my criticism holds for personal pro-theism as well.
25 Since God is by definition morally good, I will simply speak of his agency from here on out, instead of his "morally good agency."
26 It's crucial to keep in mind that the good of privacy in this scenario is not to be attributed to God's agency: the good of privacy is not something that God brings about by his actions or that is the result of God existing. And so the good of privacy is not attributed to God's existence and cannot be used to support impersonal pro-theism.
27 Or, following Nagasawa 2017, we might say that God possesses the maximal consistent set of great-making properties.
28 The bulk of Plantinga's chapter is spent arguing that the best possible worlds contain incarnation and atonement, which require sin and therefore evil. And hence God allows evil because it is necessary if there is to be incarnation and atonement. I will not discuss part of his argument, since it isn't necessary for my point here. However, it is noteworthy that Hudson 2018 has argued that this specific claim of Plantinga's theodicy succumbs to skeptical theism. (Hudson's argument only applies (if at all) to Plantinga's theodicy, not to the above argument that I consider.)
29 Though, as we saw earlier, Penner and Lougheed's argument for impersonal pro-theism does fall prey to skeptical theism.
30 Thanks to Adriane Hendricks and Kirk Lougheed for comments on this chapter. And thanks especially to G.L.G.—Colin Patrick Mitchell—for particularly insightful comments.

Bibliography

Adams, Marilyn McCord. (1999), *Horrendous Evils and the Goodness of God*. Ithaca: Cornell University Press.

Alston, William. (1991), "The Inductive Argument from Evil and the Human Cognitive Condition," *Philosophical Perspectives* 5: 29–67.

Bergmann, Michael. (2001), "Skeptical Theism and Rowe's New Evidential Argument from Evil," *Nous* 35: 278–96.

Bergmann, Michael. (2009), "Skeptical Theism and the Problem of Evil," in T. Flint and M. Rea, *The Oxford Handbook of Philosophical Theology*, pp. 375–99 Oxford: Oxford University Press.

Bergmann, Michael. (2012), "Common Sense Skeptical Theism," in *Reason, Metaphysics, and Mind: New Essays on the Philosophy of Alvin Planting*, edited by Kelly James Clark and Michael Rea, pp. 9–37. Oxford: Oxford University Press.

Collins, Robin. (2013), "The Connection-Building Theodicy," in *The Blackwell Companion to the Problem of Evil*, edited by J. P. McBrayer and D. Howard-Snyder, pp. 222–35. Malden: Wiley-Blackwell.

Cullison, Andrew. (2014), "Two New Versions of Skeptical Theism," in *Skeptical Theism: New Essays*, edited by Trent Dougherty and Justin McBrayer, pp. 250–63. Oxford: Oxford University Press.

Davis, Stephen. (2014), "On Preferring that God Not Exist: A Dialogue," *Faith and Philosophy* 31 (2): 143–59.

Dougherty, Trent. (2008), "Epistemological Considerations Concerning Skeptical Theism," *Faith and Philosophy* 25 (2): 172–76.

Dougherty, Trent. (2011), "Recent Work on the Problem of Evil," *Analysis* 71: 560–73.

Dougherty, Trent. (2014), "Skeptical Theism," *The Stanford Encyclopedia of Philosophy*, (Spring 2014 Edition), edited by E. N. Zalta. URL=https://plato.stanford.edu/archives/spr2014/entries/skeptical-theism/.

Durston, Kirk. (2000), "The Consequential Complexity of History and Gratuitous Evil," *Religious Studies* 36 (1): 65–80.

Hasker, William. (2008), *The Triumph of God Over Evil: Theodicy for a World of Suffering*. Downers Grove: Intervarsity Press Academic.

Hendricks, Perry. (2018a), "How to be a Skeptical Theist and a Commonsense Epistemologist," *Faith and Philosophy* 35 (3): 354–55.

Hendricks, Perry. (2018b), "Sceptical Theism and the Evil-God Challenge," *Religious Studies* 54 (4): 549–61.

Hendricks, Perry. (2019), "The Nature of Skeptical Theism: Answering Non-standard Objections to Skeptical Theism," *Philosophia Christi* 21 (1): 103–17.

Hendricks, Perry. (forthcoming). "Skeptical Theism Proved," *The Journal of the American Philosophical Association*.

Hendricks, Perry and Kirk Lougheed. (2019), "Undermining the Axiological Solution to Divine Hiddenness," *International Journal for Philosophy of Religion* 86 (1): 3–15.

Hudson, Hud. (2014), "The Father of Lies?" in *Oxford Studies in Philosophy of Religion*, edited by Jonathan L. Kvanvig, vol. 5, pp. 147–66. Oxford: Oxford University Press.

Hudson, Hud. (2017), *A Grotesque in the Garden*. San Bernardino: Xerxes Press.

Hudson, Hud. (2018), "Felix Culpa!" in *Two Dozen (or so) Theistic Arguments*, edited by Trent Dougherty and Jerry Walls, pp. 277–89. Oxford: Oxford University Press.

Huemer, Michael. (2007), "Compassionate Phenomenal Conservatism," *Philosophy and Phenomenological Research* 74: 30–55.

Kahane, Guy. (2011), "Should We Want God to Exist?" *Philosophy and Phenomenological Research* 82 (3): 674–96.

Kraay, Klaas J. and Chris Dragos. (2013), "On Preferring God's Non-existence," *Canadian Journal of Philosophy* 43 (2): 157–78.

Lougheed, Kirk. (2017), "Anti-Theism and the Objective Meaningful Life Argument," *Dialogue: Canadian Philosophical Review* 56 (2): 337–55.

Lougheed, Kirk. (2018), "The Axiological Solution to Divine Hiddenness," *Ratio* 31 (3): 331–41.

Lougheed, Kirk. (2019), "On How (Not) to Argue for Preferring God's Non-existence," *Dialogue: Canadian Philosophical Review* 58 (4): 677–99.

Mackie, John L. (1955), "Evil and Omnipotence," *Mind* 64: 200–12.

Nagasawa, Yujin. (2017), *Maximal God: A New Defense of Perfect Being Theism*. Oxford: Oxford University Press.

Penner, Myron. (2015), "Personal Anti-Theism and the Meaningful Life Argument," *Faith and Philosophy* 32 (3): 325–37.

Penner, Myron. (2018), "On the Objective Meaningful Life Argument: A Response to Kirk Lougheed," *Dialogue: Canadian Philosophical Review* 57 (1): 173–82.

Penner, Myron A. and Kirk Lougheed. (2015), "Pro-Theism and the Added Value of Morally Good Agents," *Philosophia Christi* 7 (1): 53–69.

Plantinga, Alvin. (2004), "Supralapsarianism, or 'O Felix Culpa,'" in *Christian Faith and the Problem of Evil*, edited by Peter van Inwagen, pp. 1–25. Grand Rapids: Eerdmanns.

Rowe, William. (1979), "The Problem of Evil and Some Varieties of Atheism," *American Philosophical Quarterly* 16 (4): 335–41.

Rubio, Daniel. (2018), "God Meets Satan's Apple: The Paradox of Creation," *Philosophical Studies* 175 (12): 2987–3004.

Stump, Eleonore. (2010), *Wandering in Darkness: Narrative and the Problem of Suffering*. Oxford: Oxford University Press.

Sullivan, Meghan. (2013), "Peter van Inwagen's Defense," in *The Blackwell Companion to the Problem of Evil*, edited by Daniel Howard-Snyder and Justin McBreyer, pp. 396–410. Oxford: Wiley-Blackwell.

Tucker, Chris. (2011), "Phenomenal Conservatism and Evidentialism in Religious Epistemology," in *Evidence and Religious Belief*, edited by K. Clark and R. VanArragon, pp. 52–76. New York: Oxford University Press.

Tucker, Chris, ed. (2013), *Seemings and Justification: New Essays on Dogmatism and Phenomenal Conservatism*. Oxford: Oxford University Press.

Van Inwagen, Peter. (1991), "The Problem of Evil, the Problem of Air, and the Problem of Silence," *Philosophical Perspectives* 5: 135–65.

Van Inwagen, Peter. (2006), *The Problem of Evil*. Oxford: Oxford University Press.

Wykstra, Stephen. (1984), "The Human Obstacle to Evidential Arguments from Suffering: On Avoiding the Evils of 'Appearance,'" *International Journal for Philosophy of Religion* 16: 73–94.

Commentary on "Skeptical Theism, Pro-theism, and Anti-theism"

Michael Almeida

Perry Hendricks aims to show that the personal (or impersonal) disvalue of God's existence provides no good reason to prefer a godless world. He takes the "objective meaningful life" argument as typical among arguments for personal anti-theism. The argument for the personal disvalue of theism goes from premise (6)—together with some auxiliary premises—to the conclusion that it is rational to prefer that God does not exist. Let O be a set of objective goods that are necessary to living a meaningful life.[1]

6. God's existence would constrain or prevent S from obtaining some of the goods in O.

(6) entails that it would be difficult, though not obviously impossible, to live a meaningful life in a world that includes God. If the argument is right, then the chances of living a meaningful life are better if we inhabit a godless world than if we inhabit a world that includes God. And since we all value a meaningful life, the argument concludes that we have personal reasons to prefer a world in which God does not exist.

Hendricks's central objection to this sort of personal anti-theistic argument is that, for all we know, there are some great goods "connected to" living meaningless lives in worlds that include God. But how would such goods affect the atheological conclusion above?

> Suppose that there is some great good *for* [an agent] x that would only obtain if God exists *and* that this good is so great that it would make x's life better for her than if she had a meaningful life. *If this is the case, then x's life would be worse for her if she had a meaningful life.* (99, my modifications)

If there is some great good for x existing exclusively in God-inhabited worlds—a good that is better than living a meaningful life—then, according to Hendricks, worlds in which God exists and x's life is meaningless are better for x than worlds in which God does not exist and x's life is meaningful. There are several more or less plausible theses that Hendricks might be defending here. Let's consider some salient options:

i. Any world in which x's life is meaningless and God exists is better for x than any world in which God does not exist and x's life is meaningful.
ii. Some worlds in which x's life is meaningless and God exists are better for x than any world in which God does not exist and x's life is meaningful.
iii. Any world in which x's life is meaningless and God exists is better for x than some worlds in which God does not exist and x's life is meaningful.
iv. Some worlds in which x's life is meaningless and God exists are better for x than some worlds in which God does not exist and x's life is meaningful.

Hendricks's closing assertion above—*if this is the case, then x's life would be worse for her if she had a meaningful life*—suggests that Hendricks believes the existence of the great good in God-inhabited worlds establishes thesis (i). But it is pretty obvious that (i) is false.

In some godless worlds w where x's life is meaningful, x enjoys the additional benefit of an everlasting and flourishing life. There are at least some permanentist worlds, for instance, that are extremely valuable for x.² In those worlds, x never goes out of existence, and in at least some of those worlds, x is never non-concrete. In those worlds x is the everlasting beneficiary of the most valuable states of affairs. The world w is no doubt better than at least some world w' in which x lives a meaningless life and enjoys a good that is greater than a meaningful life. It might also be true in w', for instance, that x suffers tremendously throughout most of his life and spends eternity in painful lamentation over his life-choices. There is, in short, a great good that x enjoys in w', but there are even greater evils that x endures in w'.

The thesis in (ii) is weaker than (i). (ii) ensures that the very best worlds for x in which God exists and life is meaningless are better for x than the very best worlds for x in which God does not exist and life is meaningful. But Hendricks's hypothesis of a great good exceeding the absolute value of a meaningless life can't establish (ii), either. There are, after all, godless worlds whose value for x is z, for any infinite cardinality z. There are, for instance, godless worlds divided into epochs of infinite duration, each including infinitely many valuable states of affairs for x and godless worlds in which x enjoys extremely valuable states of affairs in infinitely many three-dimensional hyperspaces and godless worlds in which there are uncountably many concrete universes—all including infinitely many states of affairs that are extremely valuable for x and all overlapping with respect to x.[3] In each of these worlds—and there are countless other possibilities—x enjoys benefits of some infinite cardinality. Even granting that there are also God-inhabited worlds whose value for x is z, for any infinite cardinality z, it is nonetheless true that, for any world w in which God exists whose value for x has cardinality n, there is another world in which God does not exist whose value for x has cardinality $m > n$. So it is unlikely that some worlds in which x's life is meaningless and God exists are better for x than any world in which God does not exist and x's life is meaningful.

The thesis in (iii) is more likely to be true. For any world in which x's life is meaningless and God exists there is some world that is worse for x in which God does not exist and x's life is meaningful. But the truth of (iii) provides x with no reason at all to prefer a world in which God exists, since the converse of (iii) is also likely to be true. For any world in which x's life is meaningful and God does not exist there is some world that is worse for x in which God does exist and x's life is meaningless. So x has a reason to prefer a God-inhabited world only if he doesn't. Therefore x doesn't have a reason to prefer a God-inhabited world.[4]

Let's consider finally the thesis in (iv). According to (iv) there are some God-inhabited worlds that are better for x than some godless worlds. (iv) is very likely to be true, but is (iv) sufficient to establish that x has good reason to prefer God-inhabited world? William Rowe, Michael Peterson, and John Hick—defenders of the standard approach to gratuitously evil states of affairs—urge that the answer is yes. The meaninglessness of life is a justified evil for x, on this account, and provides x with no reason to prefer a godless world. Here is Michael Peterson's principle adjusted to personal justification:

> An evil is justified [for x] if and only if it is necessary to the existence of some actual or possible greater good [for x], or to the prevention or elimination of some greater evil [for x]; an evil is gratuitous [for x] if it bears no such relations. (Peterson 1982, 96ff)[5]

According to the standard approach, the intrinsic evil of a meaningless life is non-gratuitous for x just in case some world in which x leads a meaningless life x also enjoys a greater good. If some God-inhabited worlds in which x leads a meaningless life are better for x than some godless worlds in which x leads a meaningful life, then, on the standard view, the meaninglessness of x's life is a justified evil. x has no reason to prefer a godless world to a God-inhabited world.

But the standard position won't help the case against preferring a godless world, since that view makes *every* intrinsically evil state of affairs S non-gratuitous for x, even in cases where x can prevent S without leaving things overall worse. Suppose, for instance, that x is suffering from some preventable illness, S. We know that if x had prevented S, x would thereby have prevented a greater good, since there is guaranteed to be some very valuable world w for x that includes S. If x had prevented S then x would have prevented the greater good, w. On the standard account, S is non-gratuitous for x—that is, x has no reason to prefer that S not obtain—despite the fact that it would have been better for x had x prevented S. That cannot be right.

There is good reason to reject the standard position and there is therefore good reason to reject the idea that thesis (iv) entails that x has no reason to prefer a godless world to a God-inhabited world. The fact that some worlds in which x's life is meaningless and God exists are better than some worlds in which God does not exist and x's life is meaningful does not (perhaps obviously does not) entail that x has no reason to prefer a godless world.

Notes

1. See Lougheed 2017.
2. For more on permanentism and temporaryism see Williamson 2013; Ed Zalta and Bernard Linsky 1994. See also Deasy 2018.
3. See Lewis 1986; Hudson 2006 and; Almeida, 2008.
4. The inference here is $A \supset {\sim}A \vdash {\sim}A$. Of course this thesis doesn't provide x with a reason to prefer a godless world, either.
5. See Peterson 1981, 2008. For a similar principle, see Hick 1978, 1991. For an alternative (but equivalent) principle, see Rowe 1979.

Bibliography

Almeida, Michael. (2008), *The Metaphysics of Perfect Beings*. London: Routledge.

Deasy, Daniel. (2018), "Philosophical Arguments against the A-Theory," *Pacific Philosophical Quarterly* 99 (2): 270–92.

Hick, John. (1978), *Evil and the God of Love*, 2nd edn. London: MacMillan Press.

Hick, John. (1991), "Reply," in *Problems in the Philosophy of Religion: Critical Studies of the Work of John Hick*, edited by H. Hewitt, pp. 134–37. London: MacMillan Press.

Hudson, Hud. (2006), *The Metaphysics of Hyperspace*. Oxford: Oxford University Press.

Lewis, David. (1986), *On the Plurality of Worlds*. Oxford: Blackwell.

Lougheed, Kirk. (2017), "Anti-Theism and the Objective Meaningful Life Argument," *Dialogue: Canadian Philosophical Review* 56 (2): 337–55.

Michael Peterson. (1982), *Evil and the Christian God*. Grand Rapids: Baker Book House.

Peterson, Michael. (1981), "The Inductive Problem of Evil," *Journal of the American Scientific Affiliation* 33: 82–87.

Peterson, Michael. (2008), "C.S. Lewis on the Necessity of Gratuitous Evil," in *C. S. Lewis as Philosopher: Truth, Goodness, and Beauty*, edited by D. Baggett, G. Habermas, and J. Walls, pp. 175–94. Downers Grove: InterVarsity Press.

Rowe, William. (1979), "The Problem of Evil and Some Varieties of Atheism," *American Philosophical Quarterly* 16: 335–41.

Williamson, Timothy. (2013), *Modal Logic as Metaphysics*. Oxford: Oxford University Press.

Zalta, Ed and Bernard Linsky. (1994), "In Defense of the Simplest Quantified Modal Logic," in *Philosophical Perspectives* 8: *Logic and Language*, edited by J. Tomberlin, pp. 431–58. Atascadero: Ridgeview Press.

Commentary on "Skeptical Theism, Pro-theism, and Anti-theism"

Travis Dumsday

Hendricks provides a series of clear and interesting arguments to the effect that if the core proposition of Michael Bergmann's version of skeptical theism is adopted, then recent arguments in favor of both personal and impersonal *anti-theism* are rendered problematic, while at the same time personal and impersonal *pro-theism* are left untouched. In my opinion, this last claim is very plausible; that is, the Plantingian argument in favor of impersonal pro-theism concisely summarized by Hendricks is compelling, as is Hendricks's own point that this Plantingian pro-theism is entirely compatible with Bergmann's version of skeptical theism. However, I do have minor concerns with respect to the other three views considered by Hendricks. I call them "minor" because they are idiosyncratic—they will likely only worry those who hold similar philosophical views to my own. Nevertheless, I will indulge myself by briefly laying them out.

It seems to me that the central idea supporting both the incompatibility of Bergmann's skeptical theism with anti-theism (personal and impersonal) and also its compatibility with personal pro-theism is an explicit claim about theism and the afterlife: namely, that an eternity in loving union with God would be an unsurpassable good. Thus, in responding to a revised form of Lougheed's (2017) "meaningful life argument" for personal anti-theism, Hendricks writes as follows:

> Those who hold this view may consider a different example: suppose that S's life is meaningful, and that if God exists, her life will lack meaning. Suppose, however, that if God exists, S will spend eternity with him in heaven. In such a case, S's life would lack meaning if God exists, but she'd also gain an eternal and pleasant afterlife. In such a case, S's life would be better if God exists; she should prefer that God exists even though it would mean that her life lacks meaning. And this shows that a meaningful life is not an unsurpassable good: an eternal and good afterlife is more valuable than a meaningful life. (102)

Here Hendricks is relying on the theistic prospect of a pleasant afterlife, functioning here as an unsurpassable good that can outweigh any *forfeited* goods (like meaning or privacy or autonomy) that might be referenced in support of personal anti-theism. In a related vein, in the next section (addressing impersonal anti-theism) he writes, "If there's any serious candidate for an unsurpassable anti-theistic good, I don't know of it. I leave it to the impersonal anti-theist to produce one" (104). In other words, whereas theism supplies a good candidate for an unsurpassable good (eternal life in loving union with an infinitely good God) anti-theism can at best supply only comparatively puny goods, goods which are easily overtaken by the specified unsurpassable theistic good. This core point about the afterlife comes up once again in Hendricks's section on personal pro-theism:

> However, there's an alternative way to establish personal pro-theism that *isn't* vulnerable to skeptical theism. The way to do so is to identify a good for

> some persons that is unsurpassable for them. While I argued above that none of the purported anti-theistic goods are candidates for being unsurpassable goods for some persons (or for the world), the same isn't true for at least one pro-theistic good, namely, the good of being in union with God; if God exists, some persons will have union with him. To be in union with God is to have one's will aligned with God's will and to have communion with him. (105)

This claim about theism and a positive afterlife is thus crucial for his overarching case. Two more brief quotes to this effect:

> This shouldn't be understood as my inferring from their being no goods that we know of that are greater for a person than union with God to the conclusion that there is no such good. Rather, I'm saying that this appears to be an unsurpassable good for persons, and there aren't any goods for persons that can be plausibly thought to be more valuable than it. (105)

In footnote 23 he adds: "If one could show that it's surpassable or not a plausible candidate for an unsurpassable good for persons, then skeptical theism might undermine it. But, again, this hasn't been done" (111).

My two minor worries revolve around the central role assigned to the claim that an afterlife with God would be an unsurpassable good. The first is that this claim is not a claim of theism per se but specifically of *Christian* theism. A Christian can of course affirm Hendricks's statement that "if God exists, some persons will have union with him." But other forms of theism cannot, including some ancient branches of Orthodox Judaism that denied the reality of an afterlife (e.g., the Sadducees). Moreover, a purely philosophical theism developed apart from Christian revelation might well maintain either that (a) we have no adequate reason to think that there will be an afterlife, or that (b) we have no adequate reason to think that if there is an afterlife we won't be justly damned forever for our grievous sins, or perhaps that (c) we have no adequate reason to think that *if* there is an afterlife and we *won't* be damned for our sins that we *will* somehow be capable of union with God. In other words, apart from Christian revelation it is by no means immediately obvious that there is (or could be) an afterlife or that any of us would be in any way capable of the sort of union with God that Hendricks is referencing. We are finite and wicked and He is infinite and perfectly righteous, after all. (Recall that this was one of Pascal's worries about attempts at a purely philosophical theism achieved via natural theology alone: for him, a generic philosophical theism divorced from the Christian message of redemption might easily lead someone to a perfectly rational terrified despair.) Granted Hendricks could remedy this first concern simply by specifying early on that his topic of discussion is not anti-theism and pro-theism in general but rather anti-theism and pro-theism *as assessed within a Christian theological framework*. The downside of that remedy is that some parties to the debate may resist the attempt to frame the discussion in specifically Christian terms rather than in terms of generic theism.

In fairness, my first concern is really less a worry about Hendricks's valuable work here than it is an entry point to a suggestion: namely, that those engaged in the anti-theism/pro-theism literature clarify the terms of the debate. *Is* it just a discussion between metaphysical naturalism and Christian theism, or is it intended to have a broader extension? If it would be generally agreed upon that MN and CT are the only stances properly at issue in this context, then my first concern is actually no concern at all. It really just depends on what we wish to talk about. In my own contribution to this volume I indicate that the existing literature on the axiology of theism has mostly dealt with these two stances, so I can hardly fault Hendricks for adhering to that main line of discussion. Still, I am not convinced that this situation is as it should be, nor am I convinced that the majority of those with an interest in the debate would accept those as its proper terms.

My second concern is related to the first: while it seems quite true that an anti-theist *who is also an advocate of metaphysical naturalism* will not be able to come up with any goods that could conceivably function as competitors to union with God, a *non-naturalist* anti-theist could get rather creative here. Certainly, the history of religions provides options along these lines. For instance, a certain sort of atheist anti-theist non-naturalist could still believe in an afterlife, namely, one in which a person in the know could by means of ceremonial magic achieve quite exalted states of postmortem power and knowledge and beatitude, all without having to sacrifice any autonomy to the nonexistent God of classical theism. Certainly, there have been and still are movements (for instance, some branches within the Western esoteric tradition) which affirm this sort of scenario. One might of course dismiss all such movements as balmy or pernicious or both—my point is simply that if things like this are on the table as options for discussion, then Hendricks's allegedly unsurpassable good will have many potential competitors, in the form of atheist but non-naturalist visions of beatitude that their adherents would claim surpass in personal value the beatitude promised to Christians.

Commentary on "Skeptical Theism, Pro-theism, and Anti-theism"

Graham Oppy

Consider the following three claims:

Pro-theism: It would be better if God were to exist.
Anti-theism: It would be worse if God were to exist.
Skepticism: We have no good reason to think that the goods and evils we know are connected to some instance of evil are representative of the actual goods and evils that are connected to that instance of evil.

Perry Hendricks argues that there is an asymmetry between pro-theism and anti-theism: only the former is consistent with skepticism.

Since I think that pro-theism and anti-theism are both trivial (necessary) truths—counterfactual conditionals with impossible antecedents—I think that Hendricks's asymmetry claim is false: there is no difference between pro-theism and anti-theism when it comes to consistency with any other claim. So long as the other claim is consistent, then pro-theism and anti-theism are both consistent with it; if the other claim is inconsistent, then pro-theism and anti-theism are both inconsistent with it. (What if, instead, we took pro-theism to be the claim that it would be worse if God were not to exist, and anti-theism to be the claim that it would be better if God were not to exist? These counterfactual conditionals have necessarily true antecedents; they can only be true if their consequents are necessarily true. So, I think, they are both necessarily false. Again, there is no asymmetry of the kind that Hendricks claims to detect.)

Hendricks offers three reasons "for everyone" to accept skepticism: (1) considerations about human cognitive limitations; (2) considerations of analogies between God/human and parent/child relationships; and (3) considerations about "inscrutable" states of affairs, that is, "states of affairs we know nothing significant about." Consider the following principle:

Skepticism*: We have no good reasons for thinking that the evaluative considerations that we know bear on the evaluation of an entity are representative of the actual evaluative considerations that bear on the evaluation of that entity.

It seems to me that the arguments that Hendricks offers for skepticism are no worse arguments for skepticism*. If his arguments ought to persuade everyone to accept skepticism, then they ought also persuade everyone to accept skepticism*. But Hendricks himself rejects skepticism*; he takes God to provide a counterexample to it. So, I think, he should be less sanguine about the strength of the case that he makes for skepticism.

For what it is worth, I think that skepticism and skepticism* are both false. I think that there is good reason to suppose that the kind of naturalism that I endorse holds of necessity. But, if the kind of naturalism that I endorse holds of necessity, then the goods and evils we know are connected to instances of evil *are* representative of the actual goods and evils that are connected to those instances of evil, and the evaluative considerations that we know bear on the evaluation of entities *are* representative of the actual evaluative considerations that bear on the evaluation of those entities.

The master argument that Hendricks gives *against* the consistency of anti-theism and skepticism goes something like this:

1. Anti-theism requires that God's existence would prevent the obtaining of certain goods without enabling the obtaining of other outweighing goods (premise).
2. Given skepticism, we cannot ever have good reason to think that, if God's existence were to prevent the obtaining of certain goods, God's existence would not enable the obtaining of other outweighing goods (premise).

   Therefore,
3. Given skepticism, we cannot have good reason to accept anti-theism (from 1, 2).

As Hendricks himself notes, at least inter alia, the second premise would be false if there were "unsurpassable anti-theistic goods." While there are various candidate goods that Hendricks supposes might be prevented by God's existence—the *meaningfulness* of particular lives, the *privacy* of particular individuals, the *autonomy* of particular individuals, and so forth—he notes that none of these is a good candidate for being an unsurpassable anti-theistic good. He then says: "If there's any serious candidate for an unsurpassable anti-theistic good, I don't know it. I leave it to the ... anti-theist to produce one" (104). But suppose that the anti-theist accepts skepticism. Then, surely, the anti-theist will say that no one is in any position to claim that there are no unsurpassable anti-theistic goods. Certainly, given skepticism, the fact that Hendricks is unable to identify any such goods is no reason at all to suppose that there are no such goods! But, more generally, given skepticism, the fact that none of us is able to identify any such goods is no reason at all to suppose that there are no such goods. If this is right, then Hendricks's master argument against the consistency of anti-theism and skepticism has a premise that he is not entitled to endorse.

The master argument that Hendricks gives *for* the consistency of pro-theism and skepticism goes something like this:

1. Even given skepticism, we can know that unending shared personal union with God is an unsurpassable good for persons (premise).
2. Even given skepticism, we can know that, if God were to exist, some people would obtain unending shared personal union with God (premise).

Therefore,

3. Even given skepticism we can have good reason to accept pro-theism (from 1, 2).

Hendricks says:

> [The view that unending shared union of loving personal relationship with God is the best thing for human beings] is plausible and *at the very least* isn't obviously false.... This shouldn't be understood as my inferring from there being no goods that we know of that are greater for a person than union with God to the conclusion that there is no such good. Rather, I'm saying that this appears to be an unsurpassable good for persons and there aren't any goods for persons that can be plausibly thought to be more valuable than it. (105)

Consider the following principle:

> *Skepticism#:* We have no good reason to think that the goods and evils we know are connected to some instance of good are representative of the actual goods and evils that are connected to that instance of good.

It seems to me that, given skepticism#, we cannot know that unending shared personal union with God is an unsurpassable good for persons. Indeed, given skepticism#, we cannot even know that unending shared personal union with God is good for persons. For, even if, giving consideration merely to the goods and evils we know, it seems to us that unending shared personal union with God is good for persons, given skepticism#, we are simply unable to assess how goods and evils of which we have no knowledge bear on unending shared personal union with God.

It also seems to me that whatever reasons we have for accepting skepticism must also be reasons for accepting skepticism#. Certainly, the kinds of considerations to which Hendricks appeals when he defends skepticism extend straightforwardly to an equal defense of skepticism#. But then, it seems, Hendricks ought to suppose that the following argument is no less acceptable than his master argument for the consistency of pro-theism and skepticism:

1. Even given skepticism#, we can know that unending shared personal union with God is an unsurpassable good for persons (premise).
2. Even given skepticism#, we can know that, if God were to exist, some people would obtain unending shared personal union with God (premise).

Therefore,

3. Even given skepticism# we can have good reason to accept pro-theism (from 1, 2).

But we have just seen that this argument is unsound; the first premise of this argument is false. If it is correct to suppose that skepticism and skepticism# are a package deal, then Hendricks's master argument for the consistency of pro-theism and skepticism fails.

There may be some value in joint consideration of the two arguments that Hendricks offers. In particular, it is worth noting his endorsement of Eleonore Stump's claim that "the worst thing for human beings is the unending absence of loving personal relationship with God." It seems plausible that the following argument should stand or fall with Hendricks's master argument for the consistency of pro-theism and skepticism:

1. Even given skepticism, we can know that unending absence of loving personal relationship with God is an unsurpassable bad for persons (premise).
2. Even given skepticism, we can know that, if God were to exist, some human beings would experience unending absence of loving personal relationship with God (premise).

Therefore,

3. Even given skepticism, we can have good reason to accept anti-theism (from 1, 2).

By Hendricks's lights, it seems that, for those particular people who would experience unending absence of loving personal relationship with God, the existence of God would be worse for them. Moreover, by Hendricks's lights, it seems that the existence of God would—or, at the very least, could—make the world worse by introducing into it instances of the very worst thing that there can be (people who experience unending absence of loving personal relationship with God). So, it seems, we can conclude, just on these grounds, that it cannot be that both parts of Hendricks's case are good: either he does not have a good argument for the inconsistency of skepticism and anti-theism or he does not have a good argument for the consistency of skepticism and pro-theism.

Reply to Commentaries on "Skeptical Theism, Pro-theism, and Anti-theism"

Perry Hendricks

1 Introduction

In my chapter, I (a) offered a brief argument for skeptical theism and (b) argued that skeptical theism undermines several arguments for anti-theism but leaves (at least some) arguments for pro-theism untouched. Michael Almeida, Travis Dumsday, and Graham Oppy raise different issues with my theses. Below, I respond to them.

2 Reply to Oppy

In my chapter, I argued in favor of the following thesis:

SKEPTICISM: We have no good reason for thinking that the goods and evils that we know are connected to some instance of evil are representative, in respect to their total value, of the actual goods and evils that are connected to said instance of evil. (97)

Oppy isn't impressed by my argument for SKEPTICISM. He attacks my argument indirectly. To do so, he first claims that the reasons I give for endorsing SKEPTICISM equally support the following thesis:

SKEPTICISM*: We have no good reason for thinking that the evaluative considerations that we know bear on the evaluation of an entity are representative of the actual evaluative considerations that bear on the evaluation of that entity.

He says that if my "arguments ought to persuade everyone to accept [SKEPTICISM], then they ought also persuade everyone to accept [SKEPTICISM*]. But Hendricks himself rejects [SKEPTICISM*]; he takes God to provide a counterexample to it. So, I think, he should be less sanguine about the strength of the case he makes for [SKEPTICISM]" (125, modifications mine) So, Oppy's objection to my argument in favor of SKEPTICISM is basically this: if my argument for SKEPTICISM is sound, then we should also endorse SKEPTICISM*. However, my belief in God's maximal goodness is (he thinks) undermined by SKEPTICISM*. And hence I have reason to reject SKEPTICISM* and therefore reason to reject SKEPTICISM.

Before proceeding, it's worth noting a minor issue with Oppy's objection: what is key in SKEPTICISM is the property that is relevant in respect to the representativeness of goods (and evils). I suggested the relevant property is *value*. However, in Oppy's portrayal of SKEPTICISM, he does not speak of value. Worse yet, he doesn't tell us what property is relevant in respect to representativeness in SKEPTICISM*. It's difficult to tell whether SKEPTICISM and SKEPTICISM* are equally supported by my arguments without this information.

But let's set this issue aside and grant that the case for SKEPTICISM and SKEPTICISM* are equally well grounded. Is it true that there is a counterexample to SKEPTICISM*? Does belief in God's maximal goodness commit me to denying SKEPTICISM*? I can't see why it would. SKEPTICISM is (only) an *inference blocker*: it renders unjustified inductive inferences from the goods we know of to the goods that there are.[1] Since SKEPTICISM* is meant to parallel SKEPTICISM, it too is (only) an inference blocker. But my belief in God's maximal goodness isn't predicated on an inductive inference, and hence it isn't vulnerable to SKEPTICISM*. In other words, SKEPTICISM* only blocks (certain) inferences, and since my belief in God's maximal goodness isn't predicated on an inference, it isn't a candidate to be blocked by SKEPTICISM*. Therefore, since my belief in God's maximal goodness isn't undermined by SKEPTICISM*, SKEPTICISM remains intact. And hence Oppy's first objection to SKEPTICISM is unsuccessful.

Oppy further claims that naturalism (or, at least, his version of it) entails that SKEPTICISM is false. It is unclear why he thinks this is so. Indeed, this appears to be false at worst and groundless at best. Consider some event E. If naturalism is true, it doesn't seem to follow that the goods and evils we know are connected to E are representative, in respect to value, of the goods and evils actually connected to it. For example, let E denote the event of Sally, who lives in 500 AD, enjoys smoking tobacco. Suppose that Sally knows of the various goods and evils immediately connected to E, for example, the pleasure she feels from smoking and the social engagement her smoking allows her to have. Now suppose Sally is a naturalist. What good reason does her naturalism give her for thinking that the goods (and evils) she knows are connected to her smoking are representative? There doesn't seem to be any good reason naturalism bestows upon her for thinking this. At the very least, the claim that naturalism gives her good reason to think this is groundless. And hence, Oppy's second objection to SKEPTICISM is unsuccessful.

Oppy also objects to my claim that SKEPTICISM undermines arguments for anti-theism. He portrays my argument as follows:

1. Anti-theism requires that God's existence would prevent the obtaining of certain goods without enabling the obtaining of other outweighing goods.
2. Given [SKEPTICISM], *we cannot ever* have good reason to think that, if God's existence were to prevent the obtaining of certain goods, God's existence would not enable the obtaining of other outweighing goods.
3. (Therefore) Given [SKEPTICISM], we cannot have good reason to accept anti-theism. (125, emphasis mine)

Oppy objects to this reasoning as follows:

> Suppose that the [anti-theist] accepts [SKEPTICISM]. Then . . . the [anti-theist] will say that no one is in any position to claim that there are no unsurpassable [anti-theistic] goods. Certainly, given [SKEPTICISM], the fact that Hendricks is unable to identify any such goods is no reason at all to suppose that there are no such goods! . . . If this is right, then Hendricks's master argument [i.e., (1)–(3)] against the consistency of [anti-theism] and [SKEPTICISM] has a premise that he is not entitled to endorse. (125–126)

I think Oppy's right here: SKEPTICISM does not entitle me to premise (2). However, the argument I gave in my chapter doesn't rely on premise (2): I never claimed that we *cannot ever* have reason to think that God's existence would bring about an outweighing good. Rather, I claimed that no purported anti-theistic goods are unsurpassable, and that SKEPTICISM prevents us from making inductive inferences that certain arguments for anti-theism want to make. This doesn't commit me to premise (2). Indeed, I think premise (2) is clearly false. For suppose that God told me that while his existence precludes certain goods, it doesn't enable the obtaining of other outweighing goods. If that were the case, then I would have good reason to think that the consequent of premise (2) is false. Since God telling me this is consistent with SKEPTICISM, premise (2) is false. But, again, the falsity of premise (2) doesn't threaten any thesis of mine, since I never endorsed or relied on it.

Lastly, Oppy considers my thesis that arguments for pro-theism are consistent with SKEPTICISM. He attributes to me the following argument:[2]

4. Even given [SKEPTICISM], we can know that unending shared personal union with God is an unsurpassable good for persons (premise).
5. Even given [SKEPTICISM], we can know that, if God were to exist, some people would obtain unending shared personal union with God (premise).
6. (Therefore) Even given [SKEPTICISM], we can have good reason to accept pro-theism (from 1, 2) (127).

I have no qualms with Oppy's reconstruction of my reasoning: I endorse (4)–(6). However, Oppy thinks that this spells trouble for my thesis. He argues that the reasons I give for endorsing SKEPTICISM equally support:

> SKEPTICISM#: We have no good reason to think that the goods and evils we know are connected to some instance of good are representative of the actual goods and evils that are connected to that instance of good. (126)

He claims that if SKEPTICISM undermines arguments for anti-theism (which I argued it does), then SKEPTICISM# undermines arguments for pro-theism. And hence there is either no asymmetry between pro-theism and anti-theism (which I claimed there is), or we now have reason to reject SKEPTICISM (since its truth would entail that arguments for pro-theism are undermined, which I have denied).

Recall that the argument for personal pro-theism I gave claimed that (roughly) everlasting union with God is an unsurpassable good for persons, and hence the existence of God would be better overall for those persons who end up having said union. I claimed that this argument does not need to rely on an inductive inference since union with God is a plausible candidate for an unsurpassable good for persons. If SKEPTICISM# parallels SKEPTICISM, as Oppy claims it does, then—to repeat a point I made above—it is an *inference blocker*. However, since this argument for personal pro-theism doesn't involve an inductive inference of the relevant type, it is untouched by SKEPTICISM#.[3] In other words, SKEPTICISM# would only threaten this argument for personal pro-theism *if* it relied on a (certain type of) inductive inference. But it doesn't rely on such an inference. And hence it isn't threatened by SKEPTICISM#. Therefore, even if Oppy is right that the case for SKEPTICISM equally supports SKEPTICISM#, this doesn't pose trouble for anything I argued in my chapter. Again, the problem with the anti-theistic arguments I examined is that they make use of purported goods that are *not* candidates for being unsurpassable, and this forced them to rely on an inference vulnerable to SKEPTICISM. Since the pro-theistic arguments I examined (with one exception) make use of plausible candidates for unsurpassable goods, they don't face this problem. And hence Oppy's objection here is unsuccessful: my thesis that there is an asymmetry between arguments for pro-theism and arguments for anti-theism remains intact.

3 Reply to Almeida

Almeida characterizes my objection to the objective meaningful life argument for anti-theism as claiming that "for all we know, there are some great goods 'connected to' living meaningless lives in worlds that include God" (116). He then considers several theses which (he thinks) I might be endorsing:

(i) Any world in which x's life is meaningless and God exists is better for x than any world in which God does not exist and x's life is meaningful.
(ii) Some worlds in which x's life is meaningless and God exists are better for x than any world in which God does not exist and x's life is meaningful.
(iii) Any world in which x's life is meaningless and God exists is better for x than some worlds in which God does not exist and x's life is meaningful.
(iv) Some worlds in which x's life is meaningless and God exists are better for x than some worlds in which God does not exist and x's life is meaningful (117).

He argues that (i) is false, and so considers the other theses. Later, he says that "Hendricks's hypothesis of a great good exceeding the absolute value of a meaningless life can't establish (ii), either" (117). Ultimately, he concludes that none of these theses will work for my argument: they are either false or too weak.

These quotes suggest that Almeida misunderstands my argument, for I never claimed anything like (i)–(iv) is true. Indeed, I will grant that none of these theses are known to be true. This does not affect what I argued in my chapter: I argued that SKEPTICISM undermines arguments for anti-theism but that (at least some) arguments for pro-theism are left unscathed by SKEPTICISM. In other words, none of what I argued hinges on whether (i)–(iv) are known to be true: my project was to show that (at least some) arguments for anti-theism are vulnerable to SKEPTICISM and that (at least some) arguments for pro-theism are not. To establish this, I sought to show that arguments for anti-theism rely on an inductive inference that is vulnerable to SKEPTICISM, while arguments for pro-theism do not. None of Almeida's criticism undermines my argument for this thesis. Hence, Almeida's criticism of my chapter is unsuccessful.

4 Reply to Dumsday

In my chapter, I outlined an argument for personal pro-theism and an argument for impersonal pro-theism that, I claimed, are not vulnerable to skeptical theism. The argument for personal pro-theism was (very roughly) that if theism is true, then at least some persons will have union with God, and that this is an unsurpassable good for them. Hence personal pro-theism is true. Dumsday rightly points out that what I say isn't true for all forms of theism: while Christian theism entails that some persons will have union with God, other forms of theism don't entail this. He says that this worry can be avoided by being clear that I'm addressing pro-theism from a Christian theological framework. However, he says, the "downside of that remedy is that some parties to the debate may resist the attempt to frame the discussion in specifically Christian terms rather than in terms of generic theism" (123). And he suggests that "those engaged in the anti-theism/pro-theism literature clarify the terms of the debate" (123).

Dumsday is right: my argument for personal pro-theism makes certain Christian theological assumptions, and therefore will have a limited scope of appeal.[4] And his call for clarity about the terms of debate is well taken. To remedy this situation, we can make finer grained distinctions: instead of just pro-theism and anti-theism,[5] we can speak of, for example, *Christian* pro-theism, *Judaic* pro-theism, *Buddhist* anti-theism, *atheistic non-naturalist* anti-theism, or *non-atheistic naturalist* anti-theism. In addition to bringing clarity to the picture, making these distinctions has the added bonus of allowing us to effectively rank worldviews, at least in terms of impersonal value. For example, suppose there is a successful argument for Christian pro-theism showing that Christian worlds are maximally valuable, and therefore equal or better than non-Christian worlds.[6] And suppose that there's a successful argument for pro-Judaic theism over atheistic and non-atheistic naturalist worlds, but not over Christian theism. Finally, suppose that there's a successful argument for atheistic non-naturalist anti-theism over non-atheistic naturalist anti-theism. If that's the case, then we can state the axiology of these worldviews as follows:

IMPERSONAL AXIOLOGICAL RANKING:
Christian worlds > Judaic worlds > atheistic non-naturalist worlds > non-atheistic naturalist worlds

This is more informative than speaking about just pro-theism and anti-theism. Additionally, it gives us a nice way to compare which of these worlds would be best: it allows us to consider which worldview we should hope to be true. For example, we might say that if Christianity is false, we ought to hope Judaism is true, and that non-atheistic naturalist worlds are the worst case scenario. Or, if one thinks that the Christian worldview is false, she might say that given the options that are live for her, she hopes our world turns out to be a Judaic one. So, I agree with Dumsday's point that more specificity in this area is a good thing. Indeed, as Dumsday illustrates in his chapter, there are other interesting worldviews (e.g., pantheism) worth thinking about. However, it is dubious to think that a list as neat as IMPERSONAL AXIOLOGICAL RANKING could ever be made: there will no doubt always be worldviews that we are unable to assign a place to (i.e., we can't tell which worlds—if any—we should prefer them to). But this shouldn't discourage us from adding to our arguments the clarity that Dumsday suggests.

Notes

1 Or, at least, this is the story skeptical theists tell. While I think this is correct, I don't have the space to defend it here. See e.g. Bergmann (2001) and (2012), Hendricks (2018a), and Hudson (2014) and (2017) for more on this.
2 While Oppy only considers the argument for personal pro-theism that I discuss, he presumably thinks the same criticism can be leveled at the argument for impersonal pro-theism that I consider.

3 The same, of course, is true for Plantinga's argument for impersonal pro-theism that I examined in Chapter 4: it doesn't rely on an inductive inference and is therefore not vulnerable to SKEPTICISM#.
4 The scope will be limited to those inclined toward Christian theism, and those who endorse other forms of theism that entail an afterlife involving union with God.
5 For the sake of simplicity, I'll ignore "personal" and "impersonal" variations.
6 Plantinga's (2004) defense of the felix culpa theodicy amounts to an argument for this thesis.

Bibliography

Bergmann, Michael. (2001), "Skeptical Theism and Rowe's New Evidential Argument from Evil," *Nous* 35: 278–96.

Bergmann, Michael. (2012), "Common Sense Skeptical Theism," in *Reason, Metaphysics, and Mind: New Essays on the Philosophy of Alvin Planting*, edited by Kelly James Clark and Michael Rea, pp. 9–37. Oxford: Oxford University Press.

Hendricks, Perry. (2018), "How to be a Skeptical Theist and a Commonsense Epistemologist," *Faith and Philosophy* 35 (3): 354–55.

Hudson, Hud. (2014), "The Father of Lies?" in *Oxford Studies in Philosophy of Religion*, edited by Jonathan L. Kvanvig, vol. 5, pp. 147–66. Oxford: Oxford University Press.

Hudson, Hud. (2017), *A Grotesque in the Garden*. San Bernardino: Xerxes Press.

Plantinga, Alvin. (2004), "Supralapsarianism, or 'O Felix Culpa,'" in *Christian Faith and the Problem of Evil*, edited by Peter van Inwagen, pp. 1–25. Grand Rapids: Eerdmanns.

5

Naturalistic Axiology

Graham Oppy

What axiological difference would—or does—the truth of best theistic big pictures make?

On my favorite accounts of casual reality and ontological modality, (1) all worlds share an initial causal history with the actual world and diverge from it only as a result of the outplaying of objective chance; (2) all worlds share the same causal laws; (3) actual causal reality is exhausted by actual natural reality; (4) there are no worlds in which there is causal evolution from an entirely natural state to a state that is not entirely natural; and (5) there are no gods in any entirely natural world (see Oppy 2018).

Given my favorite accounts of causal reality and ontological modality, what I have to say about "the axiology of theism" is short and sweet: (1) the truth of best theistic big pictures makes no axiological difference because there are no true best theistic big pictures; (2) the truth of best theistic big pictures could not make an axiological difference because there could not be true best theistic big pictures; (3) the truth of best theistic big pictures would not make an axiological difference because it could not make an axiological difference. It is not, cannot be, and would not be that the truth of best theistic big pictures has axiological import.

My response to the leading question is independent of answers to subsidiary questions: (1) What kind of axiological difference—intrinsic, instrumental, aesthetic, prudential, moral—is in view? (2) To which thing or things are we wondering whether the truth of best theistic big pictures might make an axiological difference? There are no things, and no kinds of things, and no kinds of axiological differences, such that the truth of best theistic big pictures does, or could, or would, make those kinds of axiological difference to those things or kinds of things. Furthermore, there could not be things, and kinds of things, and kinds of axiological differences, such that the truth of best theistic big pictures makes those kinds of axiological differences to those things or kinds of things.

My response to the leading question is not fully in view in the taxonomy of Klaas J. Kraay (2018). I do not agree with *pro-theists* that the existence of certain specified gods would or does make things better than they otherwise would be. I do not agree with *anti-theists* that the existence of certain specified gods would or does make things worse than they otherwise would be. I do not agree with *neutralists* that the existence of certain specified gods would or does make things neither better nor worse than they otherwise would be. I do not agree with *quietists* that, as a matter of principle, we cannot answer the question whether the existence of certain specified gods would or does make things better, or worse, or neither better nor worse, than they otherwise would be. And I do not agree with *agnostics* that, as a matter of fact, it is an open question whether the existence of certain specified gods would or does make things better, or worse, or neither better nor worse, than they otherwise would be.

Kraay's discussion of quietism does make mention of views according to which theism is logically impossible. He says that an advocate of such a view might say that, in principle, this "defeats any attempt to engage in comparative axiological analysis" (2018, 10); moreover, he suggests that anyone who takes this route is committed to the further claim that "precisifications of the comparative question are in principle unintelligible and hence impossible to answer sensibly" (2018, 9). I do not think that the leading question is unintelligible. I do not think that it is impossible to give a sensible response to the leading question. As I see it, the leading question rests on a false presupposition: it presupposes that there are—or could be—true best theistic big pictures. While this presupposition is false, it is not unintelligible. A perfectly fine response to the question is to point out that it rests on this false presupposition. Perhaps we might quibble about whether this response to the question also counts as an *answer* to it. But, if we do not count this as an answer, then we ought to broaden our taxonomy so that it takes in responses as well as answers.

A predictable reply to my response to the leading question is that we can evaluate the axiological difference that would be made by the truth of best theistic big pictures even if there cannot be true best theistic big pictures.

Replies that take this line might be developed in various directions. The aim of the coming discussion is to explore some of those directions.

1 Big Picture Axiology

Big pictures are philosophical theories of *everything*. In principle, big pictures are complete theories of logic, ontology, modality, axiology, and much more besides. In practice, big pictures are our best approximations to complete theories of logic, ontology, modality, axiology, and much more besides. Among other things, our big pictures give our best accounts of what there is, what there could have been, what value attaches to what there is, and what value would have attached to what could have been had it been actual.

Pretend that there is a standard unit of value that is common to big pictures: the *eval*. Pretend that a big picture assigns a score, in evals, to actual reality. Suppose that, according to big picture B1, actual reality scores n evals, whereas, according to big picture B2, actual reality scores m evals, where m>n. Suppose, further, that the difference in the eval scores for actual reality according to B1 and B2 is fully attributable to the fact that, whereas B1 is a naturalistic big picture, B2 is a theistic big picture. Pretend that B1 is your big picture and that you are aware that B2 is a competing big picture according to which actual reality scores more evals than it does according to B1. What consequences should this awareness have for your attitudes toward B1 and B2?

It is hard to see any reason for your awareness that actual reality scores more evals on B2 than it does on B1 to have consequences for your attitudes toward B1 and B2. As we have already noted, you think that it is metaphysically impossible that B2 is true. For all that we have said, you may also think that it is metaphysically possible that serious, rational, reflective, well-informed people believe—falsely—that B2 is true. Nonetheless, it is entirely unsurprising that someone who has a false big picture is mistaken in their assessment of the value of actual reality.

Perhaps it might be suggested that one of the virtues that we weigh when choosing between big pictures turns on the number of evals scored by actual reality. If it were true that, all else being equal, a big picture that assigns more evals to actual reality is better than a big picture that assigns fewer evals to actual reality, then someone who supposed that B1 and B2 were otherwise equal would be justified in preferring B2 to B1 on the grounds that actual reality scores more evals on B2 than it does on B1. But the Pollyanna principle—that, all else being equal, a big picture that assigns more evals to actual reality is better than a big picture that assigns fewer evals to actual reality—has absurd consequences. In particular, given the independence of the evaluative and the causal, it tells us that, where big pictures are tied with respect to all other considerations—including causal considerations—we should favor big pictures that assign maximal possible value to each evaluatively independent aspect of causal reality.

Perhaps it might be said that it is a mistake to focus on eval scores for actual reality. Pretend, as before, that there is a standard unit of value that is common to big pictures. But this time, pretend that a big picture assigns a score, in evals, to *you*. Suppose that, according to big picture B1, you score n evals, whereas, according to big picture B2, you score m evals, where m>n. Suppose, further, that the difference in the eval scores for you according to B1 and B2 is fully attributable to the fact that, whereas B1 is a naturalistic big picture, B2 is a theistic big picture. Pretend that B1 is your big picture and that you are aware that B2 is a competing big picture according to which you score more evals than you do according to B1. What consequences should this awareness have for your attitudes toward B1 and B2?

It is hard to see any reason to suppose that the answer to this question is any different from the answer to the similar question last time around. You think that it is metaphysically impossible for B2 to be true. You may also think that it is metaphysically possible that serious, rational, reflective, well-informed people believe—falsely—that B2 is true. Nonetheless, it is entirely unsurprising that someone who has a false big picture is mistaken in their assessment of *your* value. Adopting a false view of your value would not make you more valuable; rather, it would make you mistakenly think that you are more valuable than you actually are.

In the above discussion, I have explored the prospects for comparing the axiological claims of competing big pictures that disagree about what is possible without admitting impossibilities into our ontologies. In this discussion, I have assumed that naturalists can accept that *according to given theistic big pictures, there are maximally intrinsically valuable gods* without adding actual, or possible, or impossible maximally intrinsically valuable gods to their ontologies. Given the kinds of assumptions already introduced in the above discussion, naturalists can accept claims like the following: *according to my naturalistic big picture the intrinsic value of actual reality is n evals*, and *according to your theistic big picture, the intrinsic value of God is m evals*, and so forth. On the additional assumptions (a) that *according to big picture B, the value of a is k evals* entails *for some x, x=k and according to big picture B, the value of a is x*, and (b) *according to big picture B, the value of a is k evals* and *for some x, x=a* jointly entail that *for some x, x=a and according to big picture B, the value of x is k*, we get one grade of comparison of the axiological claims of competing big pictures. Moreover, and importantly, this grade of comparison of the axiological claims of competing big pictures is consistent with the further assumption that *according to big picture B, the intrinsic value of God is m evals* does not entail that *for some x, x = God and according to big picture B, the value of x is m evals*. Judicious selection of where we can quantify in to "according to big picture B" contexts gives us a grade of "big picture" involvement that perhaps even Quine (1953) could tolerate.

2 Big Picture Impossibilities

Big pictures are philosophical theories of *everything*. Some say that big pictures are not merely complete accounts of what there is, what there could have been, what value attaches to what there is, and what value would have attached to what could have been had it been actual. Some say that, in addition, big pictures are complete accounts of what there could not have been, and of the value that would have attached to what could not have been had it been actual.

Big pictures say: there is just *this* way that things are; there are just *these* ways that things could be. Since they are complete, big pictures entail that there are no other ways that things are and that there are no other ways that things could be. So, speaking loosely, any further proposals about how things are or could be are invocations of ways that things could not be. But, as the discussion in the previous section suggests, we do not need to quantify over ways that things could not be in order to make sense of this loose speech. Given that it seems that we can get by without committing ourselves to ways that things could not have been, the key question is whether there is sufficient reason to take on such commitment.

From the outset, it should be acknowledged that there are logically consistent theories of impossible objects and impossible worlds (see e.g. Barwise 1997; Berto 2010, 2013; Mortensen 1997; Nolan 1997, 2013; Jago 2014, and Vander Laan 1997, 2004). Moreover, it should be noted that friends of impossible objects and impossible worlds will include theories of impossible objects and impossible worlds in their big pictures. The question that I now wish to take up is whether *best* big pictures will include theories of impossible objects and impossible worlds, or whether they will rather make use of the kind of strategy that I employed in the discussion in the preceding section of this chapter.

3 Impossibilities in Philosophy of Religion

Some have argued that we need impossible objects and impossible worlds in order to make sense of standard disputes in philosophy of religion. I shall consider two examples: (a) Pascal's wager argument and (b) arguments from evil.

(a) *Pascal's Wager Argument*: Kahane (2012, 36) suggests that we see no problem asking comparative evaluative questions about God's existence and nonexistence in discussion of Pascal's wager argument even though we recognize that there are views on which God's existence is impossible. Kraay (2018, 4) suggests that it is a legitimate presumption of discussions of Pascal's wager argument that we can make intelligible reference to impossible objects and impossible worlds because participants in discussions of Pascal's wager argument widely take this to be so.

Nonetheless, it seems to me that we would do well to discuss Pascal's wager argument without invoking impossible objects and impossible worlds. Taking for granted the standard decision-theoretic formulation of the argument from dominating expectation, it seems to me to be perfectly appropriate for naturalists to say that it is not the case that they assign a non-zero probability to the hypothesis that God exists. Given naturalism, it is impossible that God exists, and so the hypothesis that God exists gets probability zero. Given necessitarian theism, it is necessary that God exists, and so the hypothesis that God exists gets probability 1. If a naturalist is certain of the truth of naturalism, then they give probability 0 to theism. However, if a naturalist is not certain of the truth of naturalism, then they make no probability assignments to the truth of naturalism and the truth of theism: they say only that, according to naturalism, theism gets probability 0, and according to necessitarian theism, theism gets probability 1.

If naturalists give probability 0 to theism, then Pascal's wager argument is obviously unsound. If, on the other hand, naturalists say only (a) according to naturalism, theism gets probability 0, and (b) according to necessitarian theism, theism gets probability 1, then naturalists can conclude (c) according to naturalism, Pascal's wager argument is obviously unsound, and observe (d) it is a matter for further investigation whether, according to necessitarian theism, Pascal's wager argument is sound.

If naturalists are certain of their naturalism, then Pascal's wager argument is obviously unsound. If, however, naturalists are not certain of their naturalism, then there is no wager that presents itself to them. On the one hand, there is a view that they accept—with less than certainty—*according to which* Pascal's wager argument is obviously unsound. On the other hand, there is a view that they do not accept—but which they reject with less than certainty—*according to which* our discussion to date has not ruled it out that Pascal's wager argument is sound. Even if it turns out that, according to the view they do not accept, Pascal's wager argument is sound, that does not give them the slightest reason to change their level of confidence that naturalism is true. Nothing in our discussion to this point says that naturalists ought not pursue the question whether, according to necessitarian theism, Pascal's wager argument is sound—but it does seem pretty clear that naturalist pursuit of that question is a matter of purely academic interest.

(b) *Arguments from Evil*: Kahane (2012, 36) says that discussions of "the problem of evil" appear to presuppose that we can sensibly compare what things would be like on theism and naturalism, and make coherent axiological comparisons, even though many participants in these discussions maintain that God's existence is either logically necessary or logically impossible. However, it seems to me that what is worthwhile in discussions of arguments from evil by naturalists and necessitarian theists involves no commitment to impossible objects and impossible worlds.

There are two questions that arise in connection with the assessment of big pictures.

First, for each big picture considered in isolation, there is the question whether it is subject to internal defeat. We may suppose that classical inconsistency suffices for internal defeat; we may suppose only that damaging relevant inconsistency suffices for internal defeat. However we think about logical inconsistency, we shall suppose that, given that a big picture is subject to logical inconsistency, there are derivations that exhibit the logical inconsistency. Moreover, because logical inconsistency is formal, a derivation that exhibits the logical inconsistency of a big picture requires no assumptions about the meanings of the nonlogical terms that figure in that derivation.[1]

Second, for big pictures that are not subject to internal defeat, there is the comparative question whether one big picture is more theoretically virtuous than its competitors. Since, on plausible assumptions, comparison of many big pictures reduces to many pairwise comparisons, we lose no generality if we consider the case in which two big pictures, B1 and B2, are compared for theoretical virtue. While there is more to argue about here, it is reasonable to suppose that the key question in the comparison of the theoretical virtues of B1 and B2 concerns the relative merits of the trade-offs that they make between minimizing commitments—ontological, ideological, nomological—and maximizing explanatory breadth and depth. While, in general, there is no algorithm for making such assessments, there are special cases: if B1 has fewer commitments of every kind than B2 and is nowhere bested by B2 for explanatory breadth and depth, then B1 is clearly more theoretically virtuous than B2.

Arguments from evil are intended as demonstrations that theistic big pictures are subject to internal defeat. In general, these arguments can be taken to have the following form (though, of course, this is not the form in which they are standardly presented):

1. According to theistic big picture T: $p_1, \ldots, p_n$.
2. $\{p_1, \ldots, p_n\}$ is (damagingly) inconsistent.

    Therefore,

3. Theistic big picture T is subject to internal defeat.

An argument that fits this general form is an argument from evil only if the premises include some nonredundant claims about evil and some nonredundant claims about divine attributes. In many logical systems, including classical logical systems, there are meta-theorems that link inconsistency and logical consequence; for example, in many logical systems, we have that $\{p_1, \ldots, p_n\}$ is inconsistent iff the negation of one of the p_i is derivable from all of the rest of the p_i. In standard form arguments from evil, the claim that it is not the case that God exists is allegedly derived from a bunch of claims that belong to best theistic big pictures.

The key point to note here is that there is nothing in this account that requires impossible objects and impossible worlds. From the standpoint of a critic of the given theistic big picture, commitment to the first premise does not bring with it commitment to impossible objects and impossible worlds, even though the critic supposes that some of the p_i could not possibly be true. Sure, the proponent of the theistic big picture believes things that—by the lights of the critic—cannot possibly be true; but assertion of the first premise simply does not commit the critic to impossible objects and impossible worlds. Moreover, if you are worried that the second premise brings commitments with it, you can replace it with the same claim prefixed with "According to theistic big picture T" without disrupting the validity of the argument.[2]

Some may be inclined to object that, while the above may serve as an account of what are commonly called "logical arguments from evil," it is not adequate as an account of what are commonly called "evidential arguments from evil." However, to the extent that "evidential arguments from evil" are intended to be *arguments* for the internal defeat of theistic big pictures, the above criticism holds. And, to the extent that "evidential arguments from evil" are intended to be components of the evaluation of the comparative theoretical virtues of competing big pictures, they are properly considered in the context of the assessment of comparative theoretical virtue, to which we now turn. It is important to remember that the comparative question only arises for big pictures that are *not* subject to internal defeat. From a classical standpoint, inconsistent big pictures are maximally committing; from any standpoint, it is clear that damagingly inconsistent big pictures are not maximally virtuous.

When we compare the theoretical virtues of competing big pictures, we take everything on which the competing big pictures agree to be data, and we treat everything else as theory. Data involves a host of shared theoretical commitments and a host of shared explanations; there is nothing in data that requires proponents on either side to be committing themselves to what they take to be impossible objects and impossible worlds. When we compare naturalist and necessitarian theist best big pictures, data includes a range of claims about the distribution of various kinds of suffering over time and place. By the lights of proponents on either side, it may be that proponents on the other side commit themselves to impossible objects and impossible worlds in the theoretical claims that they make in order to explain this data. But, when the theoretical costs are reckoned, we make judicious use of protective operators to ensure that no additional commitments are incurred.

So, for example, naturalists may note that, according to a given theistic big picture, much of the data about the distribution of various kinds of suffering over time and place is explained by the activities of demons. Since naturalistic big pictures involve no commitments to demons, this is a cost for those theistic big pictures that is not shared by naturalistic big pictures. If there is nothing in the data about the distribution of various kinds of suffering over time and place that is better explained on theistic big pictures than on naturalistic big pictures, and if there are no new postulations that naturalists make in order to explain this data, then, there is a point of advantage here for naturalistic big pictures relative to those theistic big pictures: there is additional commitment in the theistic big picture but no gains in explanatory breadth and depth. Again, the key point to note here is that there is nothing in this account that requires impossible objects and impossible worlds: the evaluative procedure simply considers how things are from the standpoint of the competing big pictures, and then tallies up the commitments without regard to the modal status that those commitments have from the standpoints of the competing big pictures.

4 Counter-Possibles

Some have argued that we need impossible objects and impossible worlds because there are nontrivial counter-possible conditionals. So, for example, Zagzebski (1990) claims that, although, by her lights, the following are *counter-possible* conditionals, by her lights, these conditionals are false:

1. If God were not to exist, the universe would still exist.
2. If God were not good, there would be less evil in the universe that actually is.
3. If God were to want to do evil, God would not be able to do so.

According to Zagzebski, God exists of necessity, God is good of necessity, and God does not want to do evil of necessity; so it is impossible that God not exist, and impossible that God is not good, and impossible that God wants to do evil. Nonetheless, according to Zagzebski, these conditionals are substantive falsehoods rather than mere trivial truths, and it is important that we are able to give expression to related substantive true counter-possible conditionals:

4. If God were not to exist, the universe would not exist.
5. If God were not good, there might be more evil in the universe than there actually is.
6. If God were to want to do evil, God would be able to do evil.

Some might think that it is an adequate response to point to other claims that, by Zagzebski's lights, give expression to "nearby" substantive truths. Consider:

7. Necessarily, if God had not engaged in creative activity, nothing other than God would exist.
8. Necessarily, an essentially perfectly good, essentially omniscient, and essentially omnipotent being optimizes the balance of good over evil in any universe that it creates.
9. Necessarily, there is nothing that God wants to do that God is unable to do.

Some might think that, in some cases, we can supplement this response by pointing to further claims that, roughly speaking—perhaps in concert with other evidently acceptable claims—yield the "substantive" true counter-possibles as substitution instances:

10. Necessarily, nothing that fails to exist engages in creative activity.
11. Necessarily, for any being that is not (essentially) good, and anything that that being makes that is evaluable in terms of good and evil, it is possible that that being fails to maximize the balance of good over evil in that thing.[3]

If there is no reason to suppose that we *need* nontrivial counter-possible conditionals, then it is highly doubtful that (1)–(6) are compelling examples of nontrivial counter-possible conditionals. If, for example, I accept (7) and (10), then I have a substantive syntactic route to (4), and no similar substantive syntactic route to (1). But that simply doesn't suffice to show that (1) and (4) are not both trivially true. That I can take a substantive inferential route to p, and then move on from there to $p \vee \sim p$, does not suffice to show that $p \vee \sim p$ is not merely trivially true.

There is more to say. Consider big picture disputes between necessitarian theists and necessitarian naturalists. Necessitarian theists can happily accept that, according to necessitarian naturalists, there are no gods. Necessitarian naturalists can happily accept that, according to necessitarian theists, there are nonnatural causal entities. If we accept that counter-possible conditionals are trivial, then, according to necessitarian naturalists, conditionals having as antecedent the claim that there are nonnatural causal entities are trivial but conditionals having as antecedent the claim that there are no gods are nontrivial (but true only when the claim they have as consequent is necessary); and, according to necessitarian theists, conditionals having as antecedent the claim that there are no gods are trivial but conditionals having as antecedent the claim that there are nonnatural causal entities are nontrivial (but true only when the claim that have as consequent is necessary). More broadly, any conditional that has as antecedent the claim that the necessitarian theist's big picture is true will be trivial by the lights of the necessitarian naturalist; and any conditional that has as antecedent the claim that the necessitarian naturalist's big picture is true will be trivial by the lights of the necessitarian theist. But how are we then to make sense of the dispute between necessitarian theists and necessitarian naturalists over the truth of their big pictures?

I doubt that there is a serious problem here. The parties to the dispute want to know which big picture is true. But, as I noted at the end of the previous section, the proper prosecution of that dispute nowhere requires the parties to the dispute to consider how things would be were competing big pictures true. Perhaps conceptualizing the dispute requires some ability to pretend that big pictures other than one's own are true. Perhaps, for example, pretense may be required in order to permit one to figure out how things are according to a big picture other than one's own in places that presentations of the big picture are incomplete. But that does not give us a reason to think that there is a *space* in which big pictures play the kind of role that is typically assigned to *worlds*. As I noted near the outset, big pictures are theories of everything: logic, ontology, modality, axiology, and more. Only the most minimal resources are available for assessment of big pictures. Those resources are insufficient to support a space in which big pictures play the kind of role typically assigned to worlds.[4]

5 Modeling with Impossibilities

Some have argued that we need impossible objects and impossible worlds in order to make sense of various familiar kinds of modeling tasks: modeling intentional states (Nolan 2013), modeling propositional content (Berto 2010; Jago 2014), modeling fiction (Berto 2013), modeling perceptual impossibilities (Mortensen 1997), modeling inconsistent databases (Barwise 1997), and so on. Other have argued that we need impossible objects and impossible worlds in order to make sense of familiar kinds of reasoning: reasoning about alternative logics (Brogaard and Salerno 2013), reasoning about mathematical conjectures (Nolan 1997), reasoning about metaphysical theories (Nolan 2013), and so forth. Yet others have argued that, even if it is not true that we need impossible objects and impossible worlds for these various purposes, the fact that we can press impossible objects and impossible worlds into service for such a diverse range of ends itself provides us with good reason to suppose that there are impossible objects and impossible worlds.

I am skeptical about the suggestions that we *need* impossible objects and impossible worlds for various theoretical ends. Certainly, the following things are data: people sometimes have beliefs that cannot all be true; people sometimes have desires that cannot all be satisfied; people sometimes say things that cannot be true; people sometimes tell stories that cannot be true; people sometimes receive perceptual inputs that cannot all be veridical; people sometimes reason using reductio ad absurdum; people sometimes investigate mathematical conjectures; people sometimes adopt competing metaphysical theories even though no more than one of those competing theories is even possibly true; and so on. But, as I see it, there is nothing in any of this that properly invites commitment to impossible objects and impossible worlds.

Consider a small child who sincerely believes that Santa Claus will bring her presents later on in the year. On my view, her belief cannot possibly be true. But, on my view, it is a mistake to suppose that we need an impossible object—Santa Claus—for the child's belief to be *about*, and it is another mistake to suppose that we need an impossible world—in which Santa Claus brings her presents—in order for her belief to have *content*. Broadly speaking, in my view, it is just a mistake to make additions to ontology to provide "representational content" for cases in which it seems that there is no "representational content" ready to hand.

While it is true that the child believes that Santa Claus will bring her presents, there is no thing—possible or impossible—of which she believes that *it* will bring her presents. While it is true that the child believes that Santa Claus will bring her presents, there are no worlds—possible or impossible—in which Santa Claus brings her presents that "supply the content" for the belief that she has.

Among the pressing questions that now arise, there are, for example (a) questions about the rule of accommodation and/or pretense and/or tacit prefixing in the assertibility of sentences like "Santa Claus has a white beard"; (b) questions about systematic compositional semantics for natural languages; and (c) questions concerning the semantic contribution that "Santa Claus" makes to the sentence "Virginia believes that Santa Claus will bring her presents later on in the year." In circumstances where "Santa Claus has a white beard" is assertible, this might be, for example, because (1) in the context, hearers obey the rule of accommodation and take us to be saying that, according to the relevant myth or story, Santa Claus has a white beard; or (2) because, in the context, it is clear to hearers that our sentence is tacitly prefixed with an "according to the relevant myth or story" operator; or (3) because, in the context, hearers understand that we are pretending that the relevant myth or story is true, and so, in particular, are pretending to assert a sentence in which we are pretending that the name "Santa Claus" refers to an actually existing person. If we suppose that, while "Santa Claus has a white beard" is false—because there is no Santa Claus—"Virginia believes that Santa Claus has a white beard" is true, then, to give but one example, we may have a compositional semantic theory according to which "Santa Claus" has a sense but no referent, so that positive sentences in which "Santa Claus" has extensional occurrence are all false, but some positive sentences in which "Santa Claus" has hyperintensional occurrence are true while others are false (See Oppy 1992a, 1992b, 1997).

Once we have in view considerations about the rule of accommodation, pretense, tacit prefixing, and the like, it is not hard to see how these considerations might find gainful employment in discussion of alternative logics, mathematical conjectures, metaphysical theories, and the like. Conversation between those with very different big pictures can proceed smoothly—without any invocation of impossible objects and impossible worlds—so long as the parties to the conversation are clear-headed about when and where some of the parties are relying on rules of accommodation, or recognition that they are entering into pretense, or recognition that they are making use of tacit operators, and so on.

What about the claim that, even if it is not true that we need impossible objects and impossible worlds for these various purposes, the fact that we can press impossible objects and impossible worlds into service for such a diverse range of ends itself provides us with good reason to suppose that there are impossible objects and impossible worlds? Straight up, it is worth noting that the ends are not very diverse. On the one hand, there are dramatic kinds of misrepresentation and pseudo-representation; on the other hand, there are certain kinds of formal reasoning. In both kinds of cases, the invocation of impossible objects and impossible worlds is made because, without them, there is no "representational content" ready to hand. But if, as my previous discussion suggests, we have the resources to provide equally good or better treatments of *each* of these kinds of cases without making additions to our ontology—that is, making use of resources that we deploy in a wide range of *other* cases—then we have no reason to commit ourselves to impossible objects and impossible worlds: seen from the proper perspective, the alleged "unification" afforded by impossible objects and impossible worlds disappears from view.

6 Preferences over Impossibilities

As Kraay (2018) observes, there is a subsidiary thread in recent discussions of naturalistic axiology, beginning with Kahane (2011), that considers the rationality of preferences concerning that which one takes to be impossible. Kraay (2018, 20) cites Thomas Nagel (1997, 131):

> I want atheism to be true and am made uneasy by the fact that some of the most intelligent and well-informed people I know are religious believers. It isn't just that I don't believe in God and, naturally, hope that I'm right in my belief. It's that I hope there is no God! I don't want there to be a God; I don't want the universe to be like that.

In his subsequent discussion, Kraay "gathers together sentiments like hopes, wishes and fears under the heading of preferences"; in his view, Nagel expresses a clear *preference* for God's nonexistence.[5]

I think that we do well to give separate consideration to the things that Kraay lumps together under the label "preferences." Let's start with desires. I shall assume that beliefs, desires, and intentions are the well-springs of rational action; I shall assume, further, that we act with practical reason only when our beliefs, desires, and intentions are appropriately coordinated.

Consider the following case. It's 1930. Johnny is an aspiring logician. He has arrived at a conference at which he is scheduled to present a paper that outlines a proof of the decidability of arithmetic. Johnny is looking forward to his session; he wants to present his paper to an audience that will contain many of the best logicians in the world. This is not just some passing whim; Johnny has a deep and burning desire to give this presentation, and a deep and burning desire to tell the world that arithmetic is decidable. Before his session, he goes to another scheduled talk. The presenter of this talk is Kurt Gödel. Johnny is very smart; by the time that Gödel's talk is done, Johnny recognizes that, in his talk, Gödel has proven that arithmetic is undecidable. By the end of Gödel's talk, Johnny no longer has a deep and burning desire to give his presentation; instead, because he now strongly desires not to present his paper, he cancels his scheduled session. As a direct consequence of rational changes in his beliefs, Johnny no longer has a deep and burning desire to tell the world that arithmetic is decidable; indeed, as a result of those rational changes in his belief, Johnny no longer has any desire at all to try to establish that arithmetic is decidable. As Johnny now sees it, it would be impossible for anyone to show that arithmetic is decidable.

While there are different lessons that one might draw from the case that I have just described, the key claim that I wish to extract is that, in a practically rational person, recognition of impossibility goes along with extirpation of related desires. Sure enough, before Johnny heard Gödel's talk, he wanted something that is impossible; but, after he had heard Gödel's talk, and had come to believe that what he had wanted was impossible, the desire simply disappeared. There are reasons for thinking that this lesson of Johnny's case generalizes. If beliefs aim to fit the world, and desires aim to have the world fit them, desires for the impossible simply cannot realize the aim of desires. Given the directions of fit of beliefs and desires, it is to be expected that a practically rational agent who believes that it is impossible that p will not desire that p: believing that it is impossible that p while desiring that p is straightforwardly practically irrational.

There is more to tell about Johnny's case. At the end of the day, when he has returned to his hotel room, Johnny starts to fantasize about the events of the day. He imagines himself getting up in question time and demolishing Gödel's proof. He imagines the subsequent triumphant presentation of his own paper, and the standing ovation he receives from the awed assembly of the world's leading logicians. He imagines the gathering in the pub at the end of the day where all of those logicians hang on his every word. And so on. Perhaps the fantasizing is the first step in Johnny's overcoming the serious psychic bruising that he has just undergone. Perhaps it has some other explanation. The important point about his fantasizing is that he is well aware that it is just fantasizing: he has no inclination to behave toward others in ways that depend upon his mistaking what is true according to his fantasies for actual fact. His fantasies—like his dreams—serve whatever functions they serve even if they are premised on impossibilities. But his fantasies cannot stand in for his desires as inputs to practically rational action. Where hopes and wishes shade into fantasies, it is a mistake to suppose that they are properly grouped together with desires under the label "preferences," given that preferences are taken to be inputs to rational action.

It is not obviously implausible to suppose that, while some hopes and wishes can be inputs to rational action, other hopes and wishes cannot. Some hopes and wishes are mere fantasies; other hopes and wishes are not. When we consider whether given hopes and wishes are "preferences," we need to look carefully at the context in which these hopes and wishes are located, and we need to be scrupulous in capturing their precise content. One of the characters in Davis (2014, 155) claims that it is possible to prefer something that is impossible, and offers, as an example, "the student who prefers that calculus or quantum theory be a lot simpler than they are." Should we suppose that we have here a case of rational preference for the impossible?

One question to ask is precisely what content should be assigned to the student's "preference." Is the student best understood to be expressing a preference about the content of calculus and quantum theory or about her ability to master calculus and quantum theory? If asked to speak carefully, would the student agree that her central preference is that she find it easier to master difficult subject matters like calculus and quantum mechanics than she currently does? A desire to find it easier to master difficult subject matters like calculus and quantum mechanics than one currently does is satisfiable: if you work hard enough at particular difficult subject matters, you will find it easier to master cognate difficult subject matters. Understood this way, the student has a rational desire that it is possible to satisfy. If, instead, the student has the slightly curious central desire to find calculus and quantum mechanics easier than she currently does, then the rational way for her to satisfy that desire is for her to devote a serious chunk of effort to study in cognate areas before she returns to the study of calculus and quantum mechanics. However, if the student's preference is that the content of calculus and quantum mechanics be such that, with no change in her current abilities, she can master calculus and quantum mechanics without much effort, then this preference cannot be construed as a desire that could form one of the well-springs of a rational course of action. Rather—and this brings us to the second question to ask about this case—it seems that we should take the preference to be an expression of some kind of wishful fantasy. Perhaps, for example, the student fantasizes about showing her transcript, containing scores of 100 percent for calculus and quantum mechanics, to her parents, who are hugely impressed by her mastery of such difficult subject matters, and yet also not mistaken in their assessment that these are pretty trivial subject matters.

While there is doubtless more to say, it certainly seems to me to be prima facie plausible to suppose that, given that we believe that it is impossible for there to be true theistic big pictures, it is not rational for us to have desires about the truth of theistic big pictures. Insofar as we are rational, our belief that it is impossible for there to be true theistic big pictures will extirpate any desires that we might have about the truth of theistic big pictures. Of course, this doesn't rule out fantasies or dreams in which some theistic big picture is true. Perhaps, for example, someone who supposes that it is impossible for there to be true theistic big pictures might have a fantasy in which they are Bertrand Russell coming face to face with God. God says: "So, what did you think of my universe?" "Not enough evidence, old bean, not enough evidence." But this kind of fantasizing has nothing to do with rational desires about the truth of theistic big pictures on the part of those who suppose that it is impossible that there are true theistic big pictures.

My attitudes differ from Nagel's in various respects. On the one hand, I am not made uneasy by the fact that some of the most intelligent and well-informed people I know are necessitarian theists. It is also the case that some of the most intelligent and well-informed people I know are (necessitarian) naturalists. Philosophy is rife with disagreement about what is possible. In my view, the best response that the various parties to philosophical disagreements about what is possible can make is to agree to disagree. On the other hand, I have no desire—or hope, or wish—that necessitarian theism be false. Given that I think that it is impossible that necessitarian theism be true, it would be irrational for me to desire—or hope, or wish—that necessitarian theism be false and it would also be irrational for me to desire—or hope, or wish— that necessitarian theism be true. While there are doubtless many respects in which I am irrational, this is not one of them.

Notes

1 Some may suppose that there are kinds of internal defeat that are not reducible to logical inconsistency: analytic incoherence, probabilistic incoherence, explanatory incoherence, and the like. I think that, given the completeness of big pictures, internal defeat is reducible to logical inconsistency. However, if internal defeat is not reducible to logical inconsistency, then it is straightforward to adjust the account to accommodate this complication.
2 If the inconsistency is formal, then this replacement is clearly unnecessary. If, as I suggested earlier, all inconsistency is formal, then this worry is clearly misplaced. But, even if the worry is not misplaced, it is readily dispatched.
3 Plausibly, there is no need for supplementation in the case of (9).
4 What I have said in this section includes what I would say in response to the argument of Mugg (2016).
5 Nagel could be clearer. It is one thing to not believe in God and another to believe that there is no God; one thing not to want there to be a God and another to want there to be no God; it is one thing not to want the universe to be like that and another to want the universe not to be like that. However, Nagel does say: "I hope that there is no God!" I propose that we interpret the rest of the passage in the light of this claim. Further, Nagel does not clearly commit himself to the claim that it is impossible that God exist. Perhaps, in fact, he supposes that it is possible that God exists. Nonetheless, for the purposes of the coming discussion, we can suppose—or, if necessary, pretend—that Nagel does suppose that it is impossible for God to exist.

Bibliography

Barwise, J. (1997), "Information and Impossibilities," *Notre Dame Journal of Formal Logic* 38: 488–515.

Berto, F. (2010), "Impossible Worlds and Propositions: Against the Parity Thesis," *Philosophical Quarterly* 60: 471–86.

Berto, F. (2013), "Impossible Worlds," *Stanford Encyclopedia of Philosophy*. https://plato.stanford.edu/entries/impossible-worlds/.

Brogaard, B. and J. Salerno. (2013), "Remarks on Counterpossibles," *Synthese* 190: 639–60.

Davis, S. (2014), "On Preferring that God not Exist (or that God Exist): A Dialogue," *Faith and Philosophy* 31: 143–59.

Jago, M. (2014), *The Impossible: An Essay on Hyperintensionality*. Oxford: Oxford University Press.

Kahane, G. (2011), "Should We Want God to Exist?" *Philosophy and Phenomenological Research* 82: 674–96.

Kahane, G. (2012), "The Value Question in Metaphysics," *Philosophy and Phenomenological Research* 85: 27–55.

Kraay, K. (2018), "Invitation to the Axiology of Theism," in *Does God Matter? Essays on the Axiological Consequences of Theism*, edited by K. Kraay, 1–36. London: Routledge.

Mortensen, C. (1997), "Peeking at the Impossible," *Notre Dame Journal of Formal Logic* 38: 527–34.

Mugg, J. (2016), "The Quietist Challenge to the Axiology of God: A Cognitive Approach to Counterpossibles," *Faith and Philosophy* 33: 441–60.

Nagel, T. (1997), *The Last Word*. Oxford: Oxford University Press.

Nolan, D. (1997), "Impossible Worlds: A Modest Approach," *Notre Dame Journal of Formal Logic* 38: 535–72.

Nolan, D. (2013), "Impossible Worlds," *Philosophy Compass* 8: 360–72.

Oppy, G. (1992a), "Semantics for Propositional Attitude Ascriptions," *Philosophical Studies* 67: 1–18.

Oppy, G. (1992b), "Why Semantic Innocence?" *Australasian Journal of Philosophy* 70: 153–61.

Oppy, G. (1997), "The Philosophical Insignificance of Gödel's Slingshot," *Mind* 106: 121–41.

Oppy, G. (2018), *Naturalism and Religion*. London: Routledge.

Quine, W. (1953), "Three Grades of Modal Involvement," *Proceedings of XIth International Congress of Philosophy* 14: 65–81.

Vander Laan, D. (1997), "The Ontology of Possible Worlds," *Notre Dame Journal of Formal Logic* 38: 597–620.

Vander Laan, D. (2004), "Counterpossibles and Similarity," in *Lewisian Themes: The Philosophy of David K. Lewis*, edited by F. Jackson and P. Pettit. Oxford: Oxford University Press.

Zagzebski, L. (1990), "What If the Impossible had been Actual?" in *Christian Theism and the Problems of Philosophy*, edited by M. Beatty, pp. 165–83. Notre Dame: University of Notre Dame Press.

Commentary on "Naturalistic Axiology"

Michael Almeida

The research project that focuses on the axiology of theism is primarily concerned with the axiological import of the existence or nonexistence of God. It is a historically unusual question. Only recently have philosophers of religion and others genuinely wondered whether it would be a good thing to discover that we inhabit a world that includes no God. Thomas Nagel famously volunteered his views on the subject in *The Last Word*:

> I want atheism to be true and am made uneasy by the fact that some of the most intelligent and well-informed people I know are religious believers. It isn't just that I don't believe in God and, naturally, hope that I'm right in my belief. It's that I hope there is no God! I don't want there to be a God; I don't want the universe to be like that. (1997, 130)

Nagel's attitude is directed toward what he evidently regards as an epistemically possible universe—we might say a *world*—that includes the traditional God of most contemporary philosophical discourse. Nagel's attitudes are the result of what he describes as a fear of religion. He takes for granted that he might after all discover that God exists and realize that awful fear. We might discover that God exists—despite the evident fact that Nagel is convinced that God does not exist—because the evidence available for God's nonexistence does not make it *certain* that God does not exist. Nagel might claim to know that God does not exist, but he certainly does not claim to know infallibly that God does not exist. If we were to model the propositions consistent with everything Nagel knows infallibly—or, for that matter, the propositions consistent with what we together know infallibly—we would no doubt find the proposition that God exists. So it is perfectly reasonable for Nagel to fear that God does exist.

According to Graham Oppy, on the contrary, Nagel's fear that God might exist is just irrational. God *could not* exist:

> Given my favorite accounts of causal reality and ontological modality, what I have to say about "the axiology of theism" is short and sweet: (1) the truth

of best theistic big pictures makes no axiological difference because there are no true best theistic big pictures; (2) the truth of best theistic big pictures could not make an axiological difference because there could not be true best theistic big pictures; (3) the truth of best theistic big pictures would not make an axiological difference because it could not make an axiological difference. It is not, cannot be, and would not be that the truth of best theistic big pictures has axiological import. (137)

It is natural to soften clause (2) in the quote above with a story prefix, *according to the naturalistic story*, the truth of best theistic big pictures could not make an axiological difference because there could not be true best theistic big pictures. The story prefix makes (2) almost certain to be true. There are unusual naturalistic stories—Hobbes offers one—on which God could exist, but most naturalistic stories seem to rule out that possibility and Oppy's version surely does. The prefix also ensures that the truth of (2) does not commit us one way or the other to the existence of God. Nothing embedded in the story prefix is either ontologically or propositionally committing. We can accept (2) and not thereby be committed to an ontology that does (or does not) include God and not be committed to the truth of any proposition within the scope of the prefix. It is perfectly analogous to the true assertion that, in the comic book story, Batman is Bruce Wayne, which is also ontologically and propositionally noncommitting.

But it is evident that Oppy does not understand the prefix "given my favorite account of causal reality and ontological modality" as roughly equivalent to "in the naturalistic story of causal reality and ontological modality." He rather understands the prefix as roughly equivalent to "in the *true story* of causal reality and ontological modality." And asserting a proposition prefixed with the operator "in the true story" is both ontologically and propositionally committing. Oppy intends clause (2) to be read, *according to the true story*, the truth of best theistic big pictures could not make an axiological difference because there could not be true best theistic big pictures. So, the project of axiological theism, according to Oppy, is methodologically confused:

> As I see it, the leading question rests on a false presupposition: it presupposes that there are—or could be—true best theistic big pictures. (138)

It is of course logically possible—perhaps, depending on which logic we are talking about—and mathematically and nomologically possible that a best theistic picture is true.[1] But none of these concerns what is absolutely possible. Absolute possibility concerns what is genuinely possible or what is possible full stop, and much of what is logically, mathematically, and nomologically possible is not possible, full stop. The error in the project of axiological theism, according to Oppy, is the presupposition that the best theistic pictures are absolutely possible.

So, Oppy's response to the central question in the axiology of theism is to call into question whether there is any interesting way the question can be answered:

> While this presupposition is false, it is not unintelligible. A perfectly fine response to the question is to point out that it rests on this false presupposition. Perhaps we might quibble about whether this response to the question also counts as an *answer* to it. But, if we do not count this as an answer, then we ought to broaden our taxonomy so that it takes in responses as well as answers. (138)

As far as I can tell, the methodological objection to the "leading question" of the axiology of theism is misplaced. There is an interesting way in which the question can be answered. The research project is primarily concerned with determining the axiological import of the existence or nonexistence of God. But determining the axiological import of God's existence (nonexistence) does not require the presupposition that God exists or, for that matter, the presupposition that God does not exist. All that is required to engage the leading question is that we do not possess infallible knowledge that God does not exist, and I think it's safe to say that we do not possess infallible knowledge on any metaphysical issue. It is utterly likely, frankly, that we do not possess much that even rises to the level of *fallible* knowledge concerning most metaphysical issues.

But if we do not possess infallible knowledge that theism is false, then obviously it is not *impossible to discover* that theism is true. It is consistent with our evidence that we discover that theism is true—however unlikely you might find that—so the possibility of discovering that theism is true should be assigned some positive probability.

There is an interesting way in which the leading question can be answered that does not presuppose that theism is absolutely possible. It does not presuppose that naturalism is absolutely possible, either. Further, it does not require us to countenance worlds we know to be impossible. We do not know for certain that theism is false, so we could discover that the actual world is a theistic world. Ask yourself how bad it would be to discover that the actual world is a theistic world. We know Thomas Nagel's answer. He reports that it would be the realization of a deep fear. It would be a personal loss on Nagel's view.

But we need not determine the axiology of theism along personal lines. The discovery that we live in a God-inhabited world might have great theoretical advantages. Living in a God-inhabited world might provide the resources we need for an absolute explanation of creation—the kind of explanation, as Swinburne puts it, "where everything really is explained." It might provide the resources to explain the provenance of anomalous value properties, properties that seem oddly out of place in a naturalistic world. It might provide the resources to show how freewill—that is, freewill of any sort you like—is compatible with a fully explicable universe. These, I assume, would be good things to learn.

The interesting way in which the leading question might be answered involves comparing the value of discovering that we live in a God-inhabited world with the value of discovering that we live in a God-uninhabited world. Given our total evidence, we could discover either of these alternatives. The main question of the research project is how good or bad it would be to make each discovery.

Note

1 S4 and S5 rule out the possibility of certain composite objects, for instance. See Salmon 1989. But even the weaker modal logics K_τ and K_σ rule out the possibility of certain objects. It's an open question whether any of these logics is inconsistent with traditional theism.

Bibliography

Nagel, Thomas. (1997), *The Last Word*. Oxford: Oxford University Press.
Salmon, Nathan. (1989), "On the Logic of What Might Have Been," *Philosophical Review* 98 (1): 3–3.

Commentary on "Naturalistic Axiology"

Travis Dumsday

Part of the point of Oppy's discussion is to draw attention to an overarching difficulty with the literature on the axiology of theism, from the perspective of an advocate for metaphysical naturalism: namely, it all seems rather pointless. What earthly good would it do to settle a debate between pro-theism and its competitors given that theism is metaphysically impossible? Consider for instance the following remark (where B1 = metaphysical naturalism and B2 = theism):

> Pretend that B1 is your big picture and that you are aware that B2 is a competing big picture according to which actual reality scores more evals than it does according to B1. What consequences should this awareness have for your attitudes toward B1 and B2? It is hard to see any reason for your awareness that actual reality scores more evals on B2 than it does on B1 to have consequences for your attitudes toward B1 and B2. As we have already noted, you think that it is metaphysically impossible that B2 is true. (139)

In other words, even if you "run the numbers" so to speak, and in doing so realize that our world would be better off were theism true, who cares? After all, as a settled naturalist you know that theism is not just false but metaphysically impossible. Oppy sees no utility (practical or theoretical) in engaging in this exercise. And although the preceding point is framed in terms of evaluating the axiological import of theism for reality as a whole, he reiterates the point when it comes to evaluating its import for one's own life. Thus, he writes:

> Pretend, as before, that there is a standard unit of value that is common to big pictures. But this time, pretend that a big picture assigns a score, in evals, to *you*. Suppose that, according to big picture B1, you score n evals, whereas, according to big picture B2, you score m evals, where m>n. Suppose, further, that the difference in the eval scores for you according to B1 and B2 is fully attributable to the fact that, whereas B1 is a naturalistic big picture, B2 is a theistic big picture. Pretend that B1 is your big picture and that you are aware that B2 is a competing big picture according to which you score more evals than you do according to B1. What consequences should this awareness have for your attitudes toward B1 and B2? It is hard to see any reason to

suppose that the answer to this question is any different from the answer to the similar question last time around. You think that it is metaphysically impossible for B2 to be true. (140)

Again, Oppy is at a loss to discern any use to the exercise. He therefore concludes that there is no use to the exercise.

That is the central claim of the first section of Oppy's chapter. The remainder of the piece gets into larger philosophical questions pertaining to impossible entities and how one may and may not properly engage in debates surrounding them. However, I take it that the argument of the chapter's first section is intended to be able to stand independently of the rest, and so I think I am within bounds in focusing solely on that first section. So, granting for the sake of argument that theism is impossible and metaphysical naturalism is true, I would like to reply by suggesting that Oppy may still have been a bit hasty in his assessment; that is, he may have overlooked some reasons why delving into the axiology of theism could be worthwhile for settled naturalists. At any rate I will suggest one such reason.

I maintain that the question of the utility (or not) of discussing the axiology of theism is liable to seem different to a settled naturalist as opposed to someone who is agnostic as to the truth of naturalism versus theism. To illustrate, let's consider a hypothetical agnostic. Call her "Agnes." Say Agnes is thoroughly undecided as to which way the best evidence points on the question of the truth of naturalism versus theism, and yet despite that fact she finds herself strongly wishing or hoping that theism were true. She is at first unsure as to *why* she finds herself with this wish. Maybe she wants there to be a God because the surrounding academic culture in which she is immersed is thoroughly atheistic and she has an innate tendency toward contrarianism? Or maybe her loathsome parents are committed atheists and she realizes that a religious conversion would be a way of striking back at them? Or perhaps, she thinks, her wish might be prompted by some underlying philosophical insight that she has not yet made explicit. That is, maybe there is some objectively rational grounding of her wish that theism be true. Could *that* be the case? At any rate she feels that in order to be able to pursue the question of the truth of theism versus naturalism with clarity of purpose and genuine objectivity, she must first gain some insight as to what (if any) rational grounds there might be for her seemingly spontaneous subjective preference. After all, she knows enough about psychology to be worried that her preference may end up biasing her search for the truth of the matter, perhaps leading her to ignore or downplay evidence against theism. So she wants to discover the root of that preference, and she thinks that task should include not just psychological introspection (regarding her character and family history), but investigation as to possible rational justifications for her preference.

So Agnes proceeds to reflect carefully on potential justifications for pro-theism, and to read all the relevant axiological literature. She comes to realize that some authors maintain we would be better off if theism were true because the truth of theism might open up at least some possibility for an afterlife, whereas naturalism seals our fate: death as total end. Upon reading these works she has something of a personal epiphany, recognizing that the root of her own preference for theism lay in her fear of death and the prospect of an afterlife that theism may open up. But then she continues her reading still further, and comes across the classic Epicurean argument for anti-theism: *rejection* of the reality of immaterial, supernatural deities who meddle in our lives is preferable because it cuts off the potential for postmortem punishment. This Epicurean argument leads her to a new epiphany, one that is not about her own subjective preferences but rather one that she feels provides a rational insight into objective value: namely, we would be far, far better off in a naturalist world because there is no risk for hell in a naturalist world. It is rationally preferable to forego hope of heaven in order to sidestep the risk of hell, she now thinks. Her initial preference for theism now having been overturned on account of her reflections on the axiology of theism, Agnes now returns to the *metaphysical* question of theism with what she feels is a more objective frame of mind, and comes to the conclusion that theism is not only false but impossible.

That sort of scenario seems to suggest at least a halfway decent reason for someone to delve into the axiology of theism. And by extension it provides a reason even for settled naturalists to contribute to the literature, insofar as they might wish to provide novel arguments to help people like Agnes engage in their reflections. At the very least, it is *a* reason that Oppy has not taken into consideration in his contribution.

Of course, it may be that once Agnes has realized that theism is impossible, her wish that it be true will rapidly dissipate of its own accord, which would fit in with Oppy's suggestion about apparent preferences for what turn out to be impossibilities (developed in Section 6 of his chapter). And so one might think that there was little point in her trying to obtain clarity on the axiological status of theism versus naturalism prior to determining which of them is impossible—why not just wait until the truth of the matter is determined and any irrational or untoward desires or wishes or hopes will simply take care of themselves? The answer is that for Agnes, lack of clarity about the relevant axiology was hampering her ability to engage in the relevant metaphysics; basically, the job couldn't wait. She therefore attempted to root out and expose a potential source of cognitive/affective bias in order to improve her ability to think clearly and critically about a philosophical question of considerable practical import (e.g., might she be obligated to start praying and attending church?).

How likely is it that there are enough Agneses out there to warrant philosophers (including settled naturalists) delving into the axiology of theism in order to provide these Agneses with tools for reflection? Who knows. There might at any rate be *some*, and for them a book like the present one could prove to be of use.

Commentary on "Naturalistic Axiology"

Perry Hendricks

Graham Oppy argues that a naturalist cannot prefer theism to be true. Similarly, a theist cannot prefer that naturalism be true. And this means that theists cannot be anti-theists and naturalists cannot be pro-theists. This follows from Oppy's view that one cannot prefer what one takes to be an impossibility.

In support of his claim that one cannot prefer what one takes to be impossible, Oppy tells the following story. Johnny is a logician in 1930 who sought to show arithmetic is decidable. He attended a conference where he was to present a paper purporting to show that arithmetic is decidable. However, prior to giving his presentation, Johnny attended a talk by Kurt Gödel. In Gödel's presentation, he demonstrated that it is impossible for arithmetic to be decidable. After Johnny heard Gödel's presentation, he became convinced of his (Gödel's) thesis, and came to believe that it is impossible for arithmetic to be decidable. Oppy says that Johnny no longer desires or prefers to tell others that arithmetic is decidable. And he thinks this result generalizes:

> If beliefs aim to fit the world, and desires aim to have the world fit them, desires for the impossible simply cannot realize the aim of desires. Given the direction of fit of beliefs and desires, it is to be expected that a practically rational agent who believes that it is impossible that p will not desire that p: believing that it is impossible that p while desiring that p is straightforwardly practically irrational. (152)

So, one cannot practically rationally desire what is believed to be impossible: if one desires that p while believing p is impossible, then she is practically irrational. But what is practical rationality? In explaining what practical rationality is, Oppy says:

> I shall assume that beliefs, desires, and intentions are the well-springs of rational action; I shall assume, further, that we act with practical reason only when our beliefs, desires and intentions are appropriately coordinated. (152)

So, since beliefs, desires, and intentions are the causes of rational action, we act with practical rationality only when our beliefs, desires, and intentions are "appropriately coordinated." While it is not exactly clear what appropriate coordination amounts to, it seems like Oppy is taking desires (etc.) to be appropriately coordinated just in case they are believed to be possibly fulfilled. That is, S's desire is appropriately coordinated only if S believes that it is possible to achieve the object of her desire. Crucially, preferences (of which desires are a subset) for Oppy *only* pertain to rational action: if S prefers X, then it is practically rational for her to prefer X. And hence S can only practically rationally prefer X if X is believed to be possible. So, preferences are bound up with practical rationality which, in turn, is bound up with what one believes to be possible.

Is there any good reason to think that preferences should be bound up to *practical* rationality as opposed to nonpractical rationality? (Hereafter, I will use the term "rationality" to mean "nonpractical rationality.") I see no such reason. It is legitimate to talk about practically rational preferences and rational preferences. While the former are definitionally bound to what one believes to be possible, the latter need not be bound—or, at least, it is not obvious that one can only rationally prefer what she takes to be possible. And if it is allowed that S rationally prefer what she believes to be impossible, then, for example, naturalists can be pro-theists, since they can rationally prefer theism to be true. However, it may be that Oppy thinks that practical rationality and rationality do not come apart, in which case if S is not practically rational in preferring X then she also is not rational in preferring X. Indeed, this appears to be what Oppy thinks. He says, "Insofar as we are rational, our belief that it is impossible for there to be true theistic big pictures will extirpate any desires that we might have about the truth of theistic big pictures" (154).

If Oppy is right that naturalists cannot rationally desire or prefer that theism (in his words: theistic big pictures) be true, then my above solution does not work. However, there are strong counterexamples to Oppy's case for why we should think that naturalists cannot rationally—as opposed to practically rationally—prefer theism to be true. For example, it seems as though a naturalist could rationally desire theism to be true. For suppose theism is true and that God has designed us to desire (or prefer) that he exists. If this is the case, then if a naturalist desires theism to be true, she is rational in an externalist sense, since her desire is in line with her design plan. While this counterexample is not definitive, it does give us reason to doubt Oppy's view about rational desires being bound to what is believed to be possible.

Setting the above issue aside, let us assume that preferences are bound up with practical rationality. And hence, we cannot rationally prefer what we take to be impossibilities, or *fantasies*, as Oppy calls them. If this is the case, should the axiological question about theism be focused on preferences? I doubt it. It is hard to see why we should restrict the debate to what we *prefer*. For even after we have an answer to what we should prefer, there is still a significant issue lingering in the area: namely, we might wonder which *fantasy* we *prefer** to be true, where one preferring* a state of affairs does not entail that it is possible. More specifically, let us take S preferring* X to mean that S wants X—whether X is possible or impossible—to obtain. For example, Serena and Venus Williams are sisters and professional tennis players. The sisters have played each other on multiple occasions. Their father, Roger Williams, has (presumably) watched these matches. It is impossible for both Serena and Venus to win the same match, and Roger knows this. However, as their father, he prefers* that they each win the match; he wants it to be the case that both win, though that state of affairs is impossible. While Roger might prefer that, for example, Serena win the match, he might also prefer* that they both win.

It is, I think, an interesting question of whether one prefers* theism or naturalism to be true. If Oppy is right about preferences being bound to what one takes to be possible, then it makes sense to reframe the axiological question of theism in terms of preferences*: we should consider whether we prefer* theism or naturalism to be true, instead of considering whether we prefer theism or naturalism. Moreover, nothing significant would be lost by moving from preferences to preferences* when discussing pro-theism, anti-theism, and so on. And hence if Oppy's thesis is right, it merely means we need to (slightly) reframe the discussion about the axiology of theism.

Reply to Commentaries on "Naturalistic Axiology"

Graham Oppy

In my initial contribution, I argued (a) that there is a gap in standard taxonomies of positions on the axiology of theism and (b) that my own view falls into that gap. I claimed that it would be irrational for me, given my naturalistic beliefs, to want it to be the case that God exists, and that it would also irrational for me, given my naturalistic beliefs, to want it to be the case that God does not exist. Note that I did not claim that it is always irrational for people to want impossible things—perhaps it was not irrational for Hobbes to want to square the circle—and nor did I claim that all who call themselves "naturalists" must follow my lead. It isn't always all about me; but this time, it was.

Mike Almeida says that I claim that Nagel's desire that God not exist is irrational. I was careful *not* to say this. I do not know whether Nagel supposes that it is possible that God exists; I do not know whether he supposes that there are impossible objects. And so on and so forth. As just noted, I claimed only that it would be irrational for *me*, as I am now, to want God to exist and irrational for *me*, as I am now, to want God not to exist.

I do not claim to know infallibly that God does not exist. I do not even claim to know that God does not exist. I make similar disclaimers for the full range of controversial metaphysical claims. But, standing by what I believe, I do claim that it is impossible to discover that theism is true: we could not discover that the actual world is a theistic world. There was a time when no one knew for certain that Wilkes's theorem is true. Even so, it was not true then that we could discover that Wilkes's theorem is false.

I allow that it is logically consistent with our evidence that we discover that theism is true—but I deny that we must assign positive probability to the claim that theism is true. Does that rule out my changing my mind about whether it is possible that God exists? Not at all. Like everyone else who has ever lived, I do not update my beliefs merely by conditionalization. That I now assign probability zero to the claim that God exists does not entail that I will not come reasonably to change my mind on that point. Currently, I take it that the best big picture is one according to which it is impossible that God exists. So I believe that it is impossible that God exists. So, if I assign any probability to the claim that God exists, I assign zero probability to the claim that God exists. All of this could change. My views would then be different from the views I currently hold. But there is nothing here to make me take back the claims that I advanced earlier: given what I believe, it would be irrational for me to want God to exist.

Perry Hendricks attributes to me the claim that naturalists cannot rationally desire or prefer that theism is true. He offers a counterexample: "Suppose theism is true and that God has designed us to desire (or prefer) that he exists. If this is the case, then if a naturalist desires theism to be true, she is rational in an externalist sense, since her desire is in line with her design plan" (166). But I claim only that I—and those who accept my kind of naturalism—would be irrational to desire or prefer that theism is true. And I say that, on the supposition that theism is true, whatever you like trivially follows. If theism were true and God had designed us to prefer that he exists, then (trivially) naturalists would all be irrational zombies obsessed with the wearing of pink cravats. So what? (Sure, I can *pretend* rather than suppose. But nothing is going to follow from that pretense about what I should take to be possible or about what I can rationally desire or prefer in connection with the truth of theism. If I am good at that kind of pretending, I may be able to figure out what, by their lights, some other people should take to be possible, and what, by their lights, some other people should rationally desire or prefer in connection with the truth of theism—but none of that carries lessons for what, by my lights, I should take to be possible, and for what, by my lights, I should desire or prefer in connection with the truth of theism.)

Hendricks suggests that there is a different, substantive issue that remains, concerning what we should prefer* to be true, where "S prefers* X" means that S wants X—whether X is possible or impossible—to obtain. But it should be recalled that I do not deny that people can want impossible things. What I deny is that people can reasonably want things while fully recognizing that those things are impossible. Hendricks offers the example of Roger Williams, who, we are to pretend, wants it to be the case that both of his daughters, Venus and Serena, win the singles tennis match in which they are jointly engaged, even though he is clear that it is impossible for this to be the outcome of their match. Assuming that Roger Williams is not barking mad, he wants no such thing. Sure, he wants both his daughters to do well. But, at any point in time, like everyone else, he either wants Venus to win or he wants Serena to win, or he has no preference about which one wins. He might say, "I hope they both win"; but it would be utterly uncharitable, taking him at his literal word, and to ask, "And how do you suppose that that could happen?"

Travis Dumsday takes me to have claimed that settled naturalists could have no reason for delving into the axiology of theism. He describes the interesting case of Agnes, whose lack of clarity about the relevant axiology hampers her ability to work through the relevant metaphysics. Initially, Agnes is thoroughly undecided on the question of the truth of naturalism versus theism and yet finds herself strongly hoping that theism is true. When she probes her hope, she comes to the view that rejection of God is preferable because it cuts off the potential for postmortem punishment. And then, we she returns to more metaphysical considerations, she comes to the conclusion that theism is not merely false but impossible.

I do not take myself to have argued that there is no reason for settled naturalists to contribute to the literature on the axiology of theism. More strongly, I do not take myself to have argued that there is no reason for naturalists who settled beliefs coincide with my own to contribute to the literature on the axiology of theism. After all, here I am, contributing to a book on the axiology of theism! If the position I have staked out is rationally permissible, then there was previously a gap in standard taxonomies of positions on the axiology of theism that my own view fills; and some other people may benefit from learning that this is one among the range of rationally permissible positions. If on the other hand, the position I have staked out is not rationally permissible—and if I can be brought to see that it is not rationally permissible—then I will have learned something useful that will require me to do some work repairing my views; and other people who might have been tempted to take up a similar position will be spared that particular entanglement with error.

Even if you are satisfied with my above replies, you might think that there are other lines of criticisms that should prove decisive. I am not entirely unsympathetic to that thought! I imagine that someone might argue as follows: We can treat the space of worldviews as a probability space. Moreover, we can model worldviews as sets of sentences closed under logical consequence, that is, we can model worldviews as theories. Because worldviews are theories of everything, the theories that model them will be maximally consistent, except for inconsistent worldviews that are modeled by the trivial theory. Clearly enough, the trivial theory—the theory that contains all sentences, and, in particular, all explicit contradictions—gets probability zero. But shouldn't all of the other theories in this probability space get non-zero probability?

Here is my current answer: The elements in the probability space that get non-zero probability must be possibilities—they must be things that could possibly be true. But, if we are to regard non-zero probability elements in the probability space as possibilities, then we must be able to regard those non-zero probability elements as elements in a single possibility space, that is, we must be able to regard them as co-possibilities. While some might demur at this point, it seems to me that we should insist that the correct modal logic is S5. So, we should suppose that, for any pair of elements in the space, each is possible relative to the other. But, now, consider a worldview which maintains that there is a necessarily existent God and a worldview which maintains that there is no necessarily existing God. These worldviews are not co-possible: neither is possible relative to the other. Since I believe that it is possible for there to be reasonable disagreement over the existence of a necessarily existing God, I am drawn to the following conclusion: either we cannot treat the space of worldviews as a probability space or else we are required to maintain that there are consistent—and, indeed, rationally believable—worldviews in the space of worldviews that get probability zero.

I have some sympathy for the view that we cannot treat the space of worldviews as a probability space. It seems to me that there is a perfectly good method for comparatively assessing worldviews that does not suppose that we can treat the space of worldviews as a probability space. What we do, in applying this method, is to directly compare the theoretical virtues of the worldviews in which we are interested. One worldview is better than a second just in case it makes a better fist of trading off theoretical simplicity against explanatory breadth and depth. Those who think that we can treat the space of worldviews as a probability space may well think that some Bayesian machinery effectively calculates the trade-off between theoretical simplicity (which is coded into the priors) and explanatory breadth and depth (which is coded into conditionalization). On the other hand, I doubt that any Bayesian approach of this kind can be made to work. Bayesian machinery is well suited to a whole host of theoretical tasks; but I suspect that worldview comparison is not one of those tasks.

Recommended Reading List

Azadegan, Ebrahim. (2019), "Antitheism and Gratuitous Evil," *The Heythrop Journal* 60 (5): 671–77.

Davis, S. T. (2014), "On Preferring that God Not Exist (or that God Exist): A Dialogue," *Faith and Philosophy* 31: 143–59.

Does God Matter? Essays on the Axiological Consequences of Theism. (2018), edited by Klaas J. Kraay. New York: Routledge.

Dumsday, Travis. (2016), "Anti-Theism and the Problem of Divine Hiddenness," *Sophia* 55: 179–95.

Hedberg, Trevor and Jordan Huzarevich. (2017), "Appraising Objections to Practical Apatheism," *Philosophia* 45: 257–76.

Hendricks, Perry and Kirk Lougheed. (2019), "Undermining the Axiological Solution to Divine Hiddenness," *International Journal for Philosophy of Religion* 86 (1): 3–15.

Kahane, Guy. (2011), "Should We Want God to Exist?" *Philosophy and Phenomenological Research* 82: 674–96.

Kahane, Guy. (2012), "The Value Question in Metaphysics," *Philosophy and Phenomenological Research* 85: 27–55.

Kraay, Klaas J. and Chris Dragos. (2013), "On Preferring God's Non-Existence," *Canadian Journal of Philosophy* 43: 157–78.

Linford, Dan and Jason Megill. (2018), "Cognitive Bias, the Axiological Question, and the Epistemic Probability of Theistic Belief," in *Ontology of Theistic Beliefs: Meta-Ontological Perspectives*, edited by Mirslaw Szatkowski, pp. 77–92. Berlin: de Gruyter.

Lougheed, Kirk. (2017), "Anti-Theism and the Objective Meaningful Life Argument," *Dialogue: Canadian Philosophical Review* 56 (2): 337–55.

Lougheed, Kirk. (2018a), "The Axiological Solution to Divine Hiddenness," *Ratio* 31 (3): 331–41.

Lougheed, Kirk. (2018b), "On the Axiology of a Hidden God," *European Journal for Philosophy of Religion* 10 (4): 79–95.

Lougheed, Kirk. (2019a), "Anti-Theism, Pro-Theism, and Gratuitous Evil," *Philosophia Christi* 21 (2): 101–15.

Lougheed, Kirk. (2019b), "On the Will Not to Believe and Axiological Atheism: A Reply to Cockayne and Warman," *Sophia* 58: 743–51.

Lougheed, Kirk. (2019c), "On How (Not) to Argue for Preferring God's Non-Existence," *Dialogue: Canadian Philosophical Review* 58 (4): 677–99.

Lougheed, Kirk. (2019d), "The Axiology of Theism," *Internet Encyclopedia of Philosophy*.

Luck, Morgan and Nathan Ellerby. (2012), "Should We Want God Not to Exist," *Philo* 15: 193–99.

Mawson, Tim. (2012), "On Determining How Important It Is Whether or Not there Is a God," *European Journal for Philosophy of Religion* 4: 95–105.

McLean, G. R. (2015), "Antipathy to God," *Sophia* 54: 13–24.

Moser, Paul. (2013), "On the Axiology of Theism: Reply to Klaas J. Kraay," *Toronto Journal of Theology* 29: 271–76.

Mugg, Joshua. (2016), "The Quietest Challenge to the Axiology of God: A Cognitive Approach to Counterpossibles," *Faith and Philosophy* 33: 441–60.

Penner, Myron A. (2018), "On the Objective Meaningful Life Argument: A Response to Kirk Lougheed," *Dialogue: Canadian Philosophical Review* 57 (1): 173–82.

Penner, Myron A. and Kirk Lougheed. (2015), "Pro-theism and the Added Value of Morally Good Agents," *Philosophia Christi* 17 (1): 53–69.

Rescher, Nicholas. (1990), "On Faith and Belief," in *Human Interests*, edited by Rescher Nicholas, pp. 166–78. Stanford: Stanford University Press.

Contributors

Kirk Lougheed is instructor of philosophy at the Concordia University of Edmonton, Canada. He is author (or co-author) of 23 articles and chapters. His works has been published in such places as *International Journal for Philosophy of Religion, Ratio, Religious Studies,* and *Synthese*. Kirk's first monograph is entitled *The Epistemic Benefits of Disagreement* (Springer, 2020).

Mike Almeida teaches philosophy at the University of Texas at San Antonio, USA. He's the author of *Freedom, God, and Worlds* (Oxford 2012), *Cosmological Arguments* (Cambridge, 2018), and *The Metaphysics of Perfect Beings* (Routledge, 2008). He's published many papers on the philosophy of religion, metaphysics, and logic.

Perry Hendricks is a PhD student at Purdue University, USA, and he is primarily interested in philosophy of religion, epistemology, and bioethics. His has articles accepted or published in such journals as *The Journal of the American Philosophical Association, Pacific Philosophical Quarterly,* and *American Philosophical Quarterly.*

Travis Dumsday is Associate Professor of Philosophy at Concordia University of Edmonton, Canada. He has published works in several different areas, including philosophy of science, bioethics, medieval philosophy, and Eastern Orthodox theology. He is also author of *Dispositionalism and the Metaphysics of Science* (Cambridge, 2019).

Graham Oppy is Professor of Philosophy at Monash University, Australia. He has published numerous articles and books in the philosophy of religion. His most recent book is *Atheism and Agnosticism* (Cambridge, 2018). He is also co-author of a multivolume series, *The History of Western Philosophy of Religion* (Routledge).

Index

Absolute, the 64-9, 74, 79-81, 84, 85, 87, 91
Advaita Vedanta (also Vedanta and Vendantin) 63, 64, 66, 67, 80, 81, 91, 93
agnosticism (also agnostic, agnostics) 5, 6, 14, 61, 62, 65, 66, 68-72, 80, 82, 84, 92
animism 60, 87, 90
anti-theism 5-8, 10-12, 15, 44, 61, 95-7, 110, 121, 123-7, 129, 131-4, 163
　atheistic non-naturalist 135
　impersonal 103, 104, 109, 120, 121
　narrow impersonal 96
　narrow personal 96
　non-atheistic naturalist 135
　personal 62, 93, 97, 101, 102, 109, 116, 120, 121
autonomy 11, 103-5, 107, 109, 112, 121, 123, 125

Bayesian 171

counterpossible(s) 3, 147

divine hiddenness 11

explanation(s) 25, 43, 44, 46, 47, 55, 145
　absolute 20-7, 30, 34, 35, 43-5, 52, 53, 160
　causal 25
　self (and self-caused) 28, 54, 55
evil
　gratuitous 7, 10, 100, 118, 119
　hellscapes 42, 43, 52
　the problem of 10, 51, 53, 96, 100, 103, 143

freedom (also freewill, libertarian) 21, 35, 43, 53, 71, 107, 160

governance 87-9, 93

Hindu (also Hinduism) 64, 66, 67, 93

impossible worlds (and also impossible objects) 142, 143, 145, 146, 149, 150, 151

Kahane, Guy 2, 3, 5, 8, 9, 61, 142, 143, 151
Kraay, Klaas J. 2, 5, 50, 61, 138, 142, 151, 152
　and Dragos, Chris 7, 62

Leibniz 23, 24
Lewis, David 3, 19, 20, 45, 47-9, 55

meaningful life (also meaning, meaning of life) 2, 7-10, 41, 50, 99, 101, 102, 105, 121
　argument for anti-theism, 104, 121
modal (also modality and modalized) 28, 29, 31, 51, 146
　fatalism 20, 21, 24, 25, 27, 34
　logic 171
　realism 45, 50, 54, 56
　space 34
　system 25
　theistic modal realism 20-4, 26, 27, 30, 31-4, 41-5, 48-54
multiverse 31, 42

Nagel, Thomas 2, 151, 154, 157, 160, 168
naturalism 2, 12, 13, 15, 49, 59, 60, 63, 65, 66, 69, 81, 84, 87, 89, 123, 125, 130, 131, 142, 143, 159-64, 166, 167, 169, 170
neutralism 6, 61, 65, 66, 68

panentheism 60, 64, 70
panpsychism 60, 64, 87, 90
pantheism 59, 60, 62-71, 80-7, 90-3, 135
Plantinga, Alvin (also Plantingan) 10, 27, 50, 52, 85, 97, 108, 109

pluriverse(s)   19–24, 26, 27, 30–5, 41, 42, 43, 46–53, 55, 56
polytheism   59, 60, 62, 69–72, 75, 76, 80, 82, 84–7, 90
possible world(s)   3, 4, 6, 7, 20–2, 24, 25, 30, 31, 33, 34, 41, 42, 43, 50, 51, 54, 56
privacy   8, 9, 11–13, 103–5, 107, 109, 112, 121, 125
pro-theism   5–7, 10, 14, 45, 52, 61, 62, 73, 85, 95, 121–4, 127–9, 132–5, 167
   agnostic wide impersonal   62
   impersonal   96, 106, 108–10, 120
   narrow impersonal   42, 43, 45, 52, 52, 53
   personal   96, 104–6, 120, 121
   wide impersonal   44

quietism (also quietist, quietists)   5, 6, 61, 62, 65, 69, 138

skeptical theism   96, 97, 99, 100, 102–10, 120–2, 129, 134
Spinoza (also Spinozistic)   23, 33, 34, 51, 56

ultimism   13, 60, 87, 90

www.ingramcontent.com/pod-product-compliance
Lightning Source LLC
Chambersburg PA
CBHW070641300426
44111CB00013B/2199